COUNTER VIOLENCE

YOUR GUIDE TO SURVIVING A DEADLY ENCOUNTER

COUNTER VIOLENCE

EJ Owens

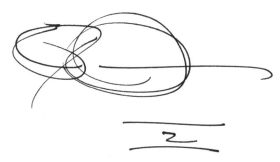

TATE PUBLISHING
AND ENTERPRISES, LLC

Published by Tate Publishing & Enterprises, LLC
127 E. Trade Center Terrace | Mustang, Oklahoma 73064 USA
1.888.361.9473 | www.tatepublishing.com

Tate Publishing is committed to excellence in the publishing industry. The company reflects the philosophy established by the founders, based on Psalm 68:11,
"The Lord gave the word and great was the company of those who published it."

Book design copyright © 2015 by Tate Publishing, LLC. All rights reserved.
Cover design by Gian Philipp Rufin
Interior design by Mary Jean Archival

Published in the United States of America

ISBN: 978-1-68028-439-3
Sports & Recreation / Shooting
14.11.19

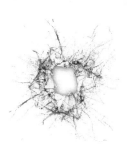

Contents

Introduction.. 7

Violence... 11

Evil... 23

Criminals.. 27

Predatory Selection... 41

Heads Up... 53

Mindset 61

Science of Gunfighting.. 71

The Fight 83

A Hero's Death... 97

Bloody Hands.. 105

Training... 113

Preparing to Attend a Shooting Class 123

Closing 133

Appendix A 137

About the Author 139

To the love of my life, Jennifer
You are my inspiration and my rock!
My children—Kaleb, Olivia, and Ethan

My sunrise and my sunset, my reason for everyday
Daddy loves you!

To my Lord and Savior Jesus Christ

Yea, though I walk through the valley of the shadow
of death, I will fear no evil.

—Psalms 23:4

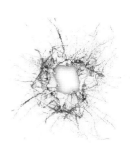

Introduction

For years now people have been asking me questions about shooting grips, stances, gun selection and situational tactics. Rarely, however, have people asked about the before or after mindset and training required to be successful in those situations. Both mindset and training are as important as the grips, the gun, and the tactics.

I try, in every case, to give my elevator speech about the "why" in regards to the "do" portion of their question. With many people I encounter there tends to be a hint of ADHD that pokes its ugly head up during these conversations because the answer being sought is not so much a matter of fact as it is a matter of context.

I can give you my elevator speech and call it a day, but as with others, I would do you a great disservice by not laying out the context. Some couldn't care less about context because they have that perfect scenario that they have been training for that ends in the same predictable manner. Others just give me that blank stare as if they haven't a clue about the real world scenarios I describe.

I find it so interesting that some are content with conversation topics about tactics and gear. These are the same people that give no thought as to whom they might fight with their tactics and gear, nor do they give any thought as to the attacker's motives or the extremes to which the attacker will go. In this book is everything I want to say to those people—and you!

This is me telling you who you are up against so that you can practice, train, and prepare should you find yourself in a deadly encounter one day. I lay out for you what evil is, how it drives the violent criminal, what can make you an easy target, and so much more. I also describe how you are going to feel emotionally should you take a life. These are topics that you don't talk about at parties, but nonetheless need to be discussed. One violent encounter will change your world or end it...forever.

This book defines for you what I stand for and what I will die for. You will need to do the same. If I were sitting right there with you, this is what I would tell you. So in a way I am there.

I wrote the chapter titled "A Hero's Death" just for you. I can't express how emotional this chapter was for me as it defines who I am and whom I continually strive to be. To see these words as they physically represent what my heart and mind feel is truly emotional. So, if when you read this, you happen to shed a few tears like I did, you're fine! Just quickly dry them before someone sees you.

I hope that after you finish this book you will pass it on to your friends and encourage them to read it as well. Then, compare notes and see how it made them feel. Let me know about it. You can email me at ejowens@legallyconcealed.org.

So, before you get started reading, let me tell you that what is in this book is what I share with all my students. I have even more that I discuss with my friends. I hope that we will meet one day soon and continue this conversation in person. Until then, the book will have to do.

In violence, we forget who we are.

—Mary McCarthy, author

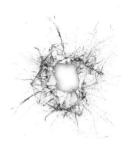

1

Violence

Definition:
vi·o·lence \\'vī-lən(t)s, 'vī-ə-\\

n.
: the use of physical force to harm someone, to damage property, etc.
: great destructive force or energy

When we hear the word *violence*, horrible pictures come to mind. The vast arrays of movies we watch contain more extravagant methods of violence than most of us are able to comprehend. Unlike the violence we watch on TV, actual violence we encounter will not have the hard-hitting, fast-paced music playing over our heads, nor will it have the off-angle, slow-motion camera shot of us as the hero boldly and successfully fighting the bad guy. More than likely, the violence we encounter will be sudden, fast, and scary.

Violence, though, can take on many different forms, and we must be able to recognize them for what they are. In our daily lives, we rarely encounter violence so we are not prepared to deal with it physically or emotionally. When the very few of us do actually encounter violence, we tend to stand in disbelief, even if for only for a moment, that it is actually happening. I want to shape for you some type of violence you might encounter should it decide that you would be the next victim.

Let's look at several types of violence. Doing so will give you a better understanding of what will be needed from you in order to survive.

Types of Violence
Physical Violence

Aggression may be physical or verbal. Verbal aggression is not considered violent. Physical aggression is not necessarily violent although it is an act intended to cause harm to the recipient (Perry, 2013). Physical aggression becomes physical violence when it involves acts with the intention of causing some degree of harm to the recipient, with death as an acceptable outcome. Physical violence may involve the use of bats, crowbars, knives, guns, or even someone's bare hands.

Anger is a frequent source of aggression, but aggressive behavior can also result from intoxication or frustration. People suffering from Alzheimer's disease may also manifest aggressive behavior as a result of diminished cognitive capacity, confusion or frustration according to many studies on this disease.

Self-mutilation, or physical violence turned against one-self, often occurs in conjunction with serious mental disorders, such as borderline personality disorder, according to WebMD.

Physical violence seems to be an act of will—that is, it is a deliberate action with the intention to harm. Guns, knives, swords, even bombs, in and of themselves, are not violent as they have no mind or will and therefore cannot choose to act. Should you encounter violence, you will most assuredly encounter physical violence.

Verbal Hostility

The child's taunt "sticks and stones may break my bones but words will never hurt me" seldom prevents the emotional distress that verbal lashes often provide. Emotional distress may become emotional abuse as verbal lashes become frequent and drawn out. Verbal lashes or outcries then become verbal hostility.

Verbal hostility (sometimes called verbal harassment or verbal abuse) is manifested through negative statements made to you, made about you within your hearing range, or made about you to others. It includes behaviors such as yelling, threatening, insulting, and bullying.

So significant is the impact of verbal hostility, the Mayo Clinic includes name-calling and insults under the category of domestic violence. Psychologists remind parents that simple put-downs—whether intentional or perceived—can have profound detrimental effects on the recipients. These profound detrimental effects continue into adulthood. Should you encounter violence, you will most assuredly encounter verbal hostility.

Nonverbal Intimidation

Nonverbal intimidation often implies the threat of violence, at least in the perception of the person on the receiving end. Stalking, for example, involves one or more forms of nonverbal intimidation, such as following the victim, planting malicious software in a victim's computer, sending unwanted gifts, and vandalizing the victim's property. A well-known example of nonverbal intimidation occurred during the movie *Fatal Attraction*, when Alex kills her victim's daughter's pet rabbit. Should you encounter violence, you are likely to encounter nonverbal intimidation.

Passive Aggression

The Mayo Clinic defines passive aggression as an indirect way of expressing displeasure or anger. Passive aggression is often generated by resentment on the part of someone who is unable or unwilling to express this resentment directly. Deliberately or subconsciously performing a task poorly is a form of passive aggression. Agreeing to perform a task but failing to do so is another. Often, procrastination is used to manifest displeasure or anger. Should you encounter violence, you are likely to find yourself utilizing passive aggression as the victim.

Types of Violent Crime

The *Federal Bureau of Investigation's Uniform Crime Report* (FBI UCR) identifies four categories of crime as violent crimes:

1. Murder
2. Forcible rape
3. Robbery
4. Aggravated assault

Let's look at what defines each of these crimes so you have a vivid understanding of what you are up against.

Murder

To help the legal system remain as fair as possible, the law actually categorizes murder in several different ways. One category used by some states is felony murder, or a murder committed during the act of another felony crime. In other states, felony murder falls under first-degree murder.

No matter if your state recognizes felony murder as a separate crime from first-degree murder or not, this is a very serious charge that can have permanent repercussions on the murderer's life. If charged with felony murder, you may have to face jail time and other serious penalties to include the death penalty.

Types of Felonies Associated with Murder

Felony murder occurs during the course of another felony. In some states, there are several felony crimes during which a killing counts as first-degree murder. These felonies include:

- Rape
- Robbery
- Burglary

- Arson
- Kidnapping

Even accidental deaths can count as felony murders in some states. For example, if you are robbing a house and the owner walks in, he or she may be frightened and try to run down the stairs. If the owner slips and falls, breaks his or her neck, and dies, you (the robber) can be held accountable for the owner's death as well as the robbery.

Forcible Rape

Rape is a type of sexual assault usually involving sexual intercourse, which is initiated by one or more persons against another person without that person's consent. The act may be carried out by physical force, coercion, abuse of authority, or against a person who is incapable of valid consent, such as one who is unconscious, incapacitated, or below the legal age of consent.

People who have been raped can be severely traumatized and may suffer from posttraumatic stress disorder (PTSD). In addition to psychological harm resulting from the act, rape may cause physical injury, or have additional effects on the victim, such as acquiring a sexually transmitted infection or becoming pregnant. Furthermore, following a rape, a victim may face violence or threats thereof from the rapist, and, in some cultures, from the victim's own family and relatives.

Robbery

Robbery is the crime of taking or attempting to take something of value by force or threat of force or by putting the victim in fear. Robbery is differentiated from other forms of theft (such as burglary, shoplifting, or car theft) by its inherently violent nature (violent nature, making it a violent crime). Whereas many lesser forms of theft are punished as misdemeanors, robbery is always a felony for this reason.

Aggravated Assault

An assault is an intentional act by one person that creates the apprehension of an imminent harmful contact. Aggravated assault is, in most jurisdictions, a stronger form of assault, often involving a deadly weapon. A person commits an aggravated assault when that person:

- causes serious bodily injury to another person with a deadly weapon;
- causes grievous bodily harm to another person, such as rape or kidnapping;
- has sexual relations with a person who is under the age of consent; or
- causes bodily harm by recklessly operating a motor vehicle.

Now that you realize crimes like those you see in *Law and Order* and *CSI* can and do happen—and they are sometimes as violent as the shows portray—let's look at violent crimes from the victim's perspective. Crimes with violence, either real or threatened, require that you the victim defend yourself physically. It may also require that you wound or take the life of your attacker. This act is called self-defense.

Right of Self-Defense

The right of self-defense, according to US law, is the right for US citizens acting on their own behalf to engage in a level of violence, called reasonable force or defensive force. This force is allowed by law for the sake of defending one's own life or the lives of others, including, in certain circumstances, the use of deadly force.

"Guns are used up to 2.5 million times each year in self-defense in the United States."-"The Armed Citizen," America's 1st Freedom, National Rifle Association, March 2013.

It is important to understand...

When the bad guy is no longer a threat (e.g., by being tackled and restrained, surrendering, or fleeing), the justification of self-defense will fail if you continue to attack or to punish beyond imposing physical restraint.

If you are at some location other than your house and taunted to a fight, accepting such a challenge and using deadly force instead of walking away, the defense of "I was only defending myself" is unlikely to save you from prosecution.

The same is true if you use force first and declare that you were protecting someone from danger. You must have a reasonable belief else the third party (the someone else) is in a position where he or she would have the right of self-defense before using force—and be able to convince the cops that your belief was correct.

Justifiable Homicide

A homicide may be considered justified if it is done to prevent a very serious crime, such as murder, rape, or armed robbery. The bad guy's intent to commit a serious crime must be clear at the time. Conversely, a homicide performed out of vengeance, or retribution for action in the past, is unlikely to be considered justifiable.

In the FBI UCR Program, justifiable homicide is defined as and limited to:

- The killing of a felon by a police officer in the line of duty.
- The killing of a felon, during the commission of a felony, by a private citizen.

When looking for similarities and differences among 277 recent justifiable homicides, the FBI found that 230 (83%) of the homicides resulted from a firearm. Of the 230 homicides, the FBI found that:

- 82 (35.7%) were known to the private citizen who used the firearm including acquaintance, boyfriend, brother, common-law husband, employee, ex-husband, ex-wife, father, friend, girlfriend, husband, in-law, neighbor, other family, other known, son, stepfather, stepson, and wife
- 130 (56.5%) were strangers
- 18 (7.8%) the relationship was unknown

In 2010, of the 230 justifiable homicides resulting from a firearm:

- 205 (89.1%) were committed by men
- 24 (10.4%) were committed by women
- 1 (0.4%) the gender of the shooter was unknown

In 2010, firearms were used in 83% of justifiable homicides (230 of 277).

- 166 (72.2%) were handguns
- 28 (12.2 %) were shotguns
- 8 (03.5 %) were rifles
- 28 (12.2 %) were firearm, type not stated

Castle Doctrine

The Castle Doctrine (or the Defense of Habitation Law) is enacted in twenty-four states. [The states are listed for you in Appendix A and is current as of 2012. Check the Internet for the latest information.] The Castle Doctrine argues that one cannot be expected to retreat from one's own home—a man's house is his castle, et domus sua cuique est tutissimum refugium (Latin for "and one's home is the safest refuge").

There have been many heated discussions about this topic. In parts of the Northeast and on the Pacific Coast, there is no Castle Doctrine legislation. Not having this protection under the law requires that homeowners retreat from their home during an active invasion and not defend their home and property lest they be prosecuted for assault or homicide. Should a homeowner shoot someone inside their home during an actual home invasion and they cannot prove that they made a concerted effort to retreat then they would, like the criminal invader, be charged with a crime. The thought from these states is that two wrongs don't make a right.

All right, so wrap your brain around this. A guy breaks into your home late at night. You get up and grab your wife and gun…now what? Oh yeah, it's time for you to jump out of a window and let him finish what he started because if you can't prove you were trying to retreat and you shoot him… wait for it…YOU GO TO JAIL TOO! I can only pray that you live in a state that has an enacted Castle Doctrine. If you don't, call your state representative and get him or her working on establishing the Castle Doctrine.

When evil men plot, good men must plan.

—Martin Luther King

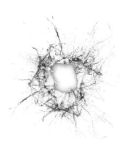

2

Evil

Definition:
e·vil [ee-vuhl]

adj.
morally wrong or bad; immoral; wicked:

Evil, according to a Judeo-Christian perspective, is any action, thought, or attitude that is contrary to the character of God. There is no moral action in the Bible that is contrary to the good inherent in God's character. Our founding fathers believed this and shaped our country's guiding principles to fight evil.

The strongest moral action against the good that defines God's character is to set one's self up as god. This action is belied in the attitude of *I can do what I want, how I want, when I want.* When this attitude imposes itself on others and does harm to them undeservingly, evil is at the door.

Understanding evil is easier when contrasted against morals. Morals are a set of personal values—your perception of what is right and what is wrong. Ethics deals with how one *ought* to think and act. Morals are the sum of *how* you think and act. When a person acts against the expectations of the society in which he or she lives, their actions are considered "evil."

Let me stop here and share with you this thought. Hopefully, it will broaden your point-of-view some. Radical Muslims following their interpretation of the Qur'an, believe that God dictates to them the killing of nonbelievers of Islam. Their morals or personal values allow killing others without defining it as murder. Chinese morals do not value human life above the good of the government. American society, however, treats murder as immoral—and even evil—as murder is outside the good defined by God's character. American society also accepts the act of killing another to preserve one's own life or the lives of others as morally acceptable, believing that is how God would react and, therefore, not evil.

Just looking at the act itself, however, can be misleading. Just as "God looks at the heart," we must also look at the intent of the person performing the act. Consider this: A woman is stopped for speeding on the interstate. Was she breaking the law? Yes! When the officer approaches the car he finds that the mother is rushing her daughter, who is actively having an asthma attack, to the hospital. In this case, the officer changes his perspective. Instead of writing the mother a speeding ticket, he moves quickly to meet the emergency needs of the daughter. Intent is key! Just as the Bible tells us that God looks not so much as to what we do, but as to why we do it, the American judicial system, created by our forefathers as a part of a Judeo-Christian society, looks closely at intent.

Here is something else for you to ponder. When tragedy happens, invariably the question of "why" comes up. "Why did he kill those innocent people?" "Why did that car accident happen?" The "why" forces us to consider intent. Although we do not want to forget the "who," in the end, it is the "why" that is most important. When we find out the "who" and then the "why," we begin the process of holding someone or some people accountable. The point here is that evil defines the intent more so than the actual act. It speaks to the reasoning one had with his or her actions.

There are many acts that our society considers as criminal, yet many criminals are not evil. They have broken laws set by society, but their actions were without intent to impose harm on others in the process. There are criminals who have broken laws relative to abusing prescription drugs, not paying taxes, even writing bad checks. Without the intent to harm others for their own personal gain, as is the case of these crimes, society does not consider these crimes "heinous" or "evil."

In the act of protecting one's home and loved ones, even strangers and their property, without the intent for personal gain, there is no evil at work. What is at work is what I call *CounterViolence*.

Countering violence aimed at you, your loved ones, or even strangers was recognized by our forefathers as a probability, a possibility, a necessity. They then insured that America's people could counter violence with the full permission of the federal government through the Second Amendment with the right to bear arms. Even with recent legislation of both the federal government and state governments to curtail the recognition and intent of those who ratified our constitution, our constitution continues to prevail.

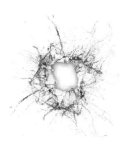

3

Criminals

Definition:
crim·i·nal (kr m -n l)

n.
: One that has committed or been legally convicted
of a crime.

adj.
: Of, involving, or having the nature of crime: criminal
abuse.

It is possible that a person can commit acts labeled "evil"
without ever being labeled a criminal first by our society.
Most things our society considers evil, however, would in
fact be a crime should the offending person be caught and
subsequently convicted. Should someone bring violence to
your doorstep, I want you to be able to size up that person and
make some sound conclusions about that person's intentions
and probable actions.

Even after centuries of study by researchers in countries around the world, the physical, psychiatric, and psychological makeup of criminals continues to be studied to find some predisposition that would lead them to do such acts. Theories about criminal behavior abound. Cesare Lombroso, an Italian criminologist, argued in 1876 that criminals are born as criminals. His research leads to later studies of why one twin becomes a criminal when the other does not. From his research in the late 1800s, today's technologies allow researchers to study neurophysiological conditions as they attempt to predefine criminals. The now-popular explanation for childhood behavioral issues, ADHD, sometimes serves as an explanation for criminal behavior.

Eysenck's Personality Theory (1977) proposes that extroverts are more likely to participate in criminal behavior than introverts. Freud laid the groundwork for studies on the effect of childhood traumatic events and family events as the instigator of criminal behavior. In 1939, Sutherland claimed that criminal behavior is learned, just as any other learning takes place. Bandura set forth an explanation for criminal behavior in 1976 that associates a person's observational learning in the family, close surroundings, and through books and television with likely criminal behavior.

Researchers in the 1970s purported the theory of *Radical Criminology*. This theory is based on the idea that no act is naturally immoral or criminal, but instead the act performed is determined to be moral or immoral, whether determined criminal or not by society. The theory favors wealthy people as it says that the wealthy are less likely to get caught after they commit a crime. *The Strain Theory*, on the other hand, proposes that poor people commit crime because it is their only way to get ahead or excuses criminal behaviors of the poor, arguing that poor people commit crimes because they can't help themselves.

Theories are plentiful. As the reader, you decide what you think influences a person, poor or wealthy, to commit a crime after you peruse crime theories in greater detail.

Individual Crime Theory

The individual crime theory group is broken down into three separate categories—Psychological, Psychiatric, and Physical.

Psychological

The psychological explanation for crime is expressed in one of these ways:

1. The criminal has a personality that was predisposed by some environmental action, which prompted an internal response from the criminal to commit the crime.
2. The criminal lacks intelligence or mental ability that would enable the criminal to have better opportunities to reach personal goals in a legitimate way or to adjust better socially.
3. The criminal cannot process the same information the way others do. This inability leads the criminal to resort to behaviors others would not even attempt due to his or her different thought patterns.
4. The criminal has character defects due to brain damage or mistreatment at home.

Psychiatric

The psychiatric explanation for crime is expressed in one of these ways:

1. The criminal never fully developed all aspects of his or her personality in a healthy and normal way and, thereby, are stuck in an immature state. This explanation points toward criminals being unable to deny themselves an impulse. This ability to deny impulses, in turn, impairs the criminal's abilities to understand why they do what they do.
2. The criminal inherited his or her criminality through biology—through genes handed off to him or her by at least one of the biological parents.

Physical

The physical explanation for crime is expressed in one of these ways:

1. The criminal has a chemical imbalance of some sort in the body.
2. The criminal has a hormonal imbalance.

Throughout history, criminologists have looked to a wide range of factors to explain why a person commits crimes. They have considered biological, psychological, physical, and even social and economic factors.

Continuing research indicates that it is, most often, a combination of these factors that brings a person to commit a crime. At some point, however, the criminal must take responsibility for his or her actions. Our justice system strives to ensure that this responsibility is taken.

Reasons

Reasons for committing a crime span elements such as greed, anger, jealously, revenge, or pride. Some people decide to commit a crime and carefully plan everything in advance to increase gain and decrease risk. Others get an adrenaline rush when successfully carrying out a dangerous crime. These people are making choices about their behavior and thus demonstrate intent. Other people commit crimes on impulse, or out of rage or fear.

The desire for material gain (money or expensive belongings) has been thought to lead to property crimes such as robberies, burglaries, white-collar crimes, and auto thefts. Property crimes are usually planned in advance. The desire for control, revenge, or power typically leads to violent crimes such as murders, assaults, and rapes. These violent crimes usually occur on impulse or the spur of the moment when emotions run high. I am certainly generalizing, but I think you get my point.

It can be argued too that domestic factors play a part in criminal behavior. Policymakers at last are coming to recognize the connection between the breakdown of American families and various social problems. The unfolding debate over welfare reform, for instance, is being shaped by the wide acceptance in recent years that children born into single-parent families are much more likely than children of intact families to fall into poverty and welfare dependence in later years. These children, in fact, face a daunting array of problems, problems that can manifest itself through acts of crime, violence, and even murder.

Evidence

A review of the empirical evidence in the professional literature of the social sciences gives us an insight into the probable root causes of crime. Consider for instance these statistics from the Heritage Foundation:

> Over the past thirty years, the rise in violent crime parallels the rise in families abandoned by fathers.
>
> State-by-state analysis by Heritage scholars indicates that a 10% increase in the percentage of children living in single parent homes leads typically to a 17% increase in juvenile crime.
>
> The type of aggression and hostility demonstrated by a future criminal often is foreshadowed in unusual aggressiveness as early as age five or six.
>
> The future criminal tends to be an individual rejected by other children as early as the first grade and goes on to form his own group of friends, often the future delinquent gang.
>
> On the other hand:
>
> Neighborhoods with a high degree of religious practice are not high crime neighborhoods.
>
> Over 90% of children from safe, stable homes do not become delinquents. By contrast only 10% of children from unsafe, unstable homes avoid crime.
>
> Criminals capable of sustaining marriage gradually move away from a life of crime after they get married.
>
> The mother's strong affectionate attachment to her child is the child's best buffer against a life of crime.
>
> The father's authority and involvement in raising his children is also a substantial and effective buffer against a life of crime.
>
> (Fagan, P. F. 1995. *The Real Root Causes of Violent Crime: The Breakdown of Marriage, Family, and Community.* Retrieved from https://www.familyfirst.org.nz/1995/03/the-real-root-causes-of-violent-crime-the-breakdown-of-marriage-family-and-community/. Source is the same for all quotes.)

The scholarly evidence, in short, suggests that at the heart of the explosion of crime in America is the loss of the capacity of fathers and mothers to be responsible in caring for the children they bring into the world. This loss of love and responsibility at the intimate levels of marriage and family has broad social consequences for children and for the greater community. The empirical evidence shows that too many young men and women from broken families tend to have a much weaker sense of connection with their neighborhood and are prone to exploit its members to satisfy their unmet needs or desires. This contributes to a loss of a sense of community and to the disintegration of neighborhoods into social chaos and violent crime.

So you see, on one hand, we have criminal acts that can be argued have external influential effects that drive persons to commit crime while thus attempting to change to person's physical environment, and on the other, we have heinous acts intended to bring about change in the person's emotional environment.

Heinous Acts

Definition:
hei·nous [heynuhs]

adj. hateful; odious; abominable; totally reprehensible:
a heinous offense.

Heinous acts are those that are deliberate in a way to cause or to contribute to lasting harm to others. They are extreme and unforgiveable by our current society. In our everyday life, we rarely encounter a true heinous act, but when we do it is even more rare to actually survive if that act is directed at us.

Once we know what a heinous act of violence really is, only then can we understand what is truly needed to counter that violence and survive.

I have talked about bringing "enough force to bear" to defeat an evil act in my DVDs and online articles (also can be found at www.legallyconcealed.org), but this is something worth repeating. You must defend yourself from heinous types of violence with enough counter violence to defeat it. Most of us are not willing to discuss openly that such a crime could happen to us or one of our loved ones, much less be prepared to enact CounterViolence should we meet violence.

There are three types of heinous acts of violence that we need to be aware of so that if someday we come face to face with one of them, we understand the criminal's mindset and what will be required of us to prevail.

- Serial Killers
- Mass Murderers
- Rapists

Serial Killer

There are a lot of questions posed at this juncture, so let's pause briefly and take a look at some facts beginning with the commonly accepted definition of the term serial killer.

The FBI Behavioral Science Unit (now the Investigative Support Unit) in Quantico, Virginia, identifies a serial killer as a person who:

- Kills three or more victims (most often one victim at a time)
- Kills over a period of time, usually days, weeks, months, or years
- Takes a cooling off period between killings

It is this latter point—the cooling off period—that separates a serial killer from a mass murderer. Ted Bundy, Jeffrey Dahmer, and Robert Ledd Yates are easily recalled serial killers. Their killings were spread over years with long cooling off periods.

Mass Murderer

The current sprees of mass murderers suggest several different psychological characteristics in this criminal type. The first characteristic is that the potential mass murderer notices the recurrent nature of mass murders taking place in any given society. His grandiose fantasy is that he wants to outperform past mass murderers. Therefore, this criminal diligently plans how he is going to surpass all previous mass murderers and become the greatest mass murderer in history. He becomes, in the most evil way possible, competitive toward other mass murderers. He uses his competitive and compulsive urges for murderous deeds rather than the normal competitive activities of society.

The second characteristic is that the mass murder often envies the people that he kills. He wants to die the same way that they do. With that thought, the mass murderer becomes both the victim and the perpetrator of murder. He sees death as a desirable solution to his problems with the world. He may even hate the world and the people in it. He may think that he is nothing and should die along with his victims. He is a person split into parts. One part wants to kill others, while the other part wishes to die. He thinks in black-and-white terms. It is either all or nothing.

A Note from EJ...

It is this point alone that should encourage law enforcement officers or the concealed carrier to engage this individual immediately. By immediately engaging him you limit his rampage on others and leaving him no choice but to move to phase 2 of his plan, which is to die. At this point, this criminal is either going to be killed by you or he is going to take his own life. Either way, he will stop killing others. Get in there!

At some point the mass murderer adopts a paradoxical vision of himself as omnipotent and grandiose, and also undeserving and of little value. He rejects people and takes the position of the loner. He justifies to himself that his position is the absolute right one and dares anyone to prove that there is another way to view the world and existence.

The mass murderer is emotionally repressed, insulated, and traumatically reverberating toward insults that were never resolved. He believes that he can do whatever he wants. He also believes no matter what he does, it is not going to change anything. So, he resorts to mass murder and probably suicide to change his sense of non-being…drastically. He spends years living in a black hole where part of him wants to do nothing and another part wants to do something.

When planning to do mass murder, this criminal believes that he is doing something others will recognize. He experiences a feeling of being God and the devil at the same time, causing a great deal of confusion. He has the omnipotent power of life and death. His defenses make him so armored that he renders it impossible for anyone to get to him. He won't and can't feel the normal range of human emotions.

A mass murderer at some point has part of his survival perception of "kill or be killed" ripped open. He proceeds to act out his fantasies onto specific and significant targets, although the targets may seem random to bystanders. It could be skin color, eye contact, the color of the clothing, a past interaction or proximity that identifies the target. Occasionally, a mass murderer will open fire on a group with no particular stimulus from someone in the group. This action, although it seems truly random, is not random. The murderer chose that site, at that time, and therefore, those people as his targets.

Murder and suicide is the mass murderer's solution to his need to be heard, understood, and accepted. His grandiosity keeps him from understanding that his very distorted thinking not only gets him rejected socially, but also alienates other people. Through mass murder and suicide, the murderer finally gets everyone's attention.

In fantasy, he gets his reckoning, but when the fantasies intensify to the point of acting out, he loses all sense of normal morality and impulse control. He doesn't question. He just acts! It is only when the mass murderer commits his atrocities that people and the media start to try to analyze and understand him. In his perverse way, he has achieved his goal.

It may be easier for you to think of a mass killing incident because all of the victims are created during one event and at a single location. For example, you might remember the Columbine School incident from 1999. More recently, you might remember the Virginia Tech campus killings in 2007 or the mass killing at the Washington Navy Yard in 2013.

A spree killing or rampage killing also creates many victims like the mass murderer. The difference is that the spree killing takes place over a short period of time in more than one location, but with no "cooling off" period. The spree killer often experiences a long period of seething anger that eventually boils to a point where the killer decides to take some form of violent action. In 2000, Richard Scott Baumhammers killed five people during a fifteen-mile journey among three townships in Pennsylvania. In 2005, Scott Moody killed five within a half-mile. In 2009, Frank Garcia killed two at a New York hospital and hours later killed a couple in their home.

Websites such as www.massacres.us offer details of such killings.

Rapist

The word *rape* itself originates from the Latin verb *rapere*, meaning to seize or take by force. In our society, we define rape as a type of sexual assault usually involving sexual intercourse, which is initiated by one or more persons against another person without that person's consent.

Rape is not about sexual gratification—it is about control. Rapists use sexual domination of another person to make themselves feel empowered. Rapists don't consider things like getting an STD and couldn't care less if they are spreading one because for them it's not about sex. Sex is merely the vehicle to achieve the ultimate goal of empowerment.

Rapists enjoy the obedience coupled with the physical signs of grief and loss their victim expresses. They take pleasure in afflicting emotional trauma and intimidation that they know will stay with their victim for life. Rapists revel in the fact that they have altered the emotional and physical state of that person forever. They are ever tied to their victim and through that they feel control. They expect a mild form of resistance leading to compliance, but are prepared to meet that little resistance with physical violence and intimidation until compliance is obtained.

The heinous criminal type we just described, the rapist, expects, and even demands, compliance. Rapists believe that their victims will ultimately comply when faced with intimidation and violence. What they do not suspect is that you will fight back and very frequently they are not prepared to counter your attack if you do fight back.

Comply and Die!

—EJ Owens, Legally Concealed

The type of resistance I am referring to for the rapist, and also for the serial killer or the mass murder, must be a full mind-and-body commitment to destroy that heinous individual at all costs—not just some kicking or a little screaming that stops upon the criminal's order. You must develop a mindset, determine in advance how you will react, give yourself permission to act as you have determined, and then train, train, train to follow through on that determination automatically and without emotion when circumstances require it.

Scream as loud as you can and get your hands on him fast. Go for the eyes, ears, and throat! Put your thumbs in his eyes until you see blood and fluid oozing down your wrists. Grab the ears and pull them off if you can. If you can, go for the throat then grab at the rigid trachea and try to pull it out. It will be very hard but understand that the simplest of force causes him to stop what he is doing to you and focus instead on the pain and the impairment of his ability to breathe. Attacking his senses will be your best chance to stop his attack. Once you have a chance to break free, it is you opportunity to run. Run to people, lots of people, screaming and yelling as loud as you can!

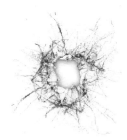

4

Predatory Selection

Definition:
pred·a·tor [pred-uh-ter, -tawr]

n.
: Zoology . any organism that exists by preying upon
other organisms.
: a predatory person–one who victimizes, plunders, or
destroys, especially for one's own gain
: one who preys upon a weaker individual

Predators have the advantage over their prey as the
predator chooses the plan, the time, and the place, as well
as the prey. Yet all their clever lures and traps depend upon
one critical factor: the naïveté of their prey. Predators see
other people as objects to exploit. Often, they know they may
need to kill an innocent person emotionally, if not literally, to
get away with the acts they want to complete. You and your
life mean nothing to them.

Types of Predators

Friendly Predator

A friendly predator will first try to get near his victim to isolate and trap, then attack. A friendly predator often appeals to your sympathy by acting in need of help or needing to ask you about something important. Many crimes begin with initially nonthreatening conversation.

Many victims, afraid to appear rude, ignore their gut feelings and become easy, naïve prey for a friendly predator. He may be good looking, well dressed, charming, and acting oh so harmless. He may have a uniform, an official-looking vehicle, or a female partner. He may hold a baby in his arms while holding a gun in his pocket. The lures predators use usually catch you by surprise and trap you in the blink of an eye. From clumsy to clever, all lures boil down to one simple warning sign—he's trying to get near you to isolate you!

Forcible Predator

A forcible predator suddenly attacks from the open or from ambush, though he may first play cat and mouse while deciding whether or not to attack. It's impossible to fully anticipate the panicky chaos of a sudden threat forcing you to make split-second decisions. Nonetheless, understanding your attacker and his plan will help you survive if it happens.

Why You?

There are a number of reasons why a violent criminal could select you. I will generalize them by breaking them down into two simple categories—Physical Traits and Environmental Situations.

A few key physical traits that are more susceptible to victimization than most include:

Lack of confidence

Your lack of projecting confidence demonstrates your perceived unwillingness to resist, thus making you an easy target in the minds of a violent attacker.

A Note from EJ...

You demonstrate confidence by looking around when you walk instead of looking at the ground or by smiling and making eye contact with those passing by.

Weak in stature

In our western society, bigger is better and perceived as putting up more resistance. Being short, skinny, or having less muscle mass than the average American citizen can make you a target if your stature is combined with a perceived lack of confidence.

A Note from EJ...

You can strengthen your stature appearance through exercise, the clothes you wear, and the confidence that you exude as you participate in your daily activities.

Shy

Generally speaking, people who are naturally shy tend to not look strangers in the eyes as they pass. They often walk as if they don't want to be noticed and avoid situations where interaction with others could be possible. This makes it easy for attackers to swoop in close as shy individuals are not as aware of their immediate surroundings as others.

A Note from EJ...

Shyness is another indicator of a lack of confidence from the predator's perception. Look around, pay attention to your surroundings, and engage others, if only with a smile or quick eye contact. Work to build confidence as predators seldom deal with confident people.

Poor Posture

How we carry ourselves says a lot about what we are willing to do should we encounter a compromising situation without ever having to say or physically demonstrate to others. Posture emulates our self-image. Slumping shoulders, shuffling feet, and hanging heads tell the criminal that we are easy prey.

A Note from EJ...

I'm sure your mother or father at some time in your life said to you, "Stand up straight," or "Hold your shoulders back." Poor posture is a neon sign to predators. Work on your posture. Standing straight demonstrates self-confidence.

Projecting Weakness

A trusting, gullible, but naïve attitude toward seemingly harmless strangers that causes a person to bare his or her soul to the person at the bar, next to you on the bus, or even in the grocery line, makes that person an easy target. In their naivety, these persons project their morals of goodness, friendliness, and belief that "since I wouldn't hurt you, you won't hurt me." Criminals love these people!

A Note from EJ...

> It is appropriate and even necessary to trust, be friendly, and engaging to those around you. Doing so, however, without first taking in your surroundings, being aware that the other person might actually harm you (date rape, for instance), and without thinking how much information about yourself you may be giving to someone who might want to hurt you is foolish. Don't be foolish. Look...Think...and then Act!

Here are a few key environmental situations that could subject you victimization:

Preoccupied With Something

When you are preoccupied with performing a task like loading groceries into your car or herding your children through a busy parking lot, you are simply unaware of your surroundings. This state of preoccupation allows criminals to advance on your position, placing them in a strategic location to dominate you. If your hands are full, you are not likely to defend yourself in time. If your headphones are on, you are not likely to be aware of someone advancing on you. If you are deep in a heated conversation on the phone while standing outside your car, again, you are not likely to realize someone is sizing you up for an attack.

Nowhere to Run

Violent criminals look for targets of opportunity. As in the animal kingdom, predators like to ambush their prey. They look for environmental bottlenecks that physically trap their victims. For example, if you attend a baseball or football game and park in an unlit field or yard several blocks away, getting to or getting into your car would provide the perfect opportunity for a carjacking. The same would be true if you park in a parking garage away from stairs or other means of immediate egress as your retreat is now futile.

Collateral Damage

Predators look for you to be in a situation that could prevent you from resisting their demands. A popular situation that predators look for is the threat of collateral damage. Collateral damage in this context implies that you have something to lose that is greater than the demands of the attacker. Should you put up resistance, for example, the predator may threaten that someone else may get hurt or killed. As a result, you allow the predator to take what he wants in order to prevent the threat from becoming a reality.

An example of this collateral damage approach is easily made with a mother (or father) with small children. When faced with a threat in such a situation, a mother's (or father's) immediate response is "whatever it takes to protect my kids." While considering the protection of the kids, however, you often forsake your own safety. Your reasoning is that if you comply with the predator the children will be unharmed.

A Note from EJ…

You cannot reason with or beg a predator—you must outmaneuver him.

Predator's Goals and Desires

It's simple! You have something he wants!

- Money
- Valuables

- Vehicle
- Weapons
- Drugs
- Control
- Sex

...to name a few!

Mental State

It's about selfishness...the different manifestations of criminal behavior is just a matter of style.

—Stanton Samenow, PhD

While everyone, to some degree or another, is selfish, criminals, whether violent and angry or just angry, take selfishness to extremes. There are thousands upon thousands of books on crime, violence, criminology, and criminal psychology. These books contain a lot of theories about the motivations of criminals. Let it be said that the theories purported by these books were developed by academia and medical personnel after interviewing and observing criminals from a position of influence over the criminals' immediate future (e.g., the psychologists were in a position to influence whether or not the criminal would be released or imprisoned). The relative positions of these professionals and researchers were controlled and therefore safe.

As influencers of the criminal's future, the criminal recognizes the need to stay in the good graces of the interviewer and often tries to "get over" on the person. This is a normal dynamic in institutionalized settings where criminals are studied. It is also why I liken the attempt to understand the violent criminals in the institutional setting to that of studying bears in the zoo. While all kinds of important zoological information can be gathered when studying bears in a zoo, you still are not dealing with the beasts in their natural habitat, nor is it likely that you will ever be on the receiving end of a bear's charge. Very few academic theories relative to the nature of the criminal mind have been developed while looking down the business end of a gun.

In the last chapter, I talked about intent. It is in the act of determining intent that leads us to the decision for the appropriate course of action. In some cases, the mere criminal act alone is justification for us to return a violent, defensive response without having determined intent first. An example of this is a guy pulling a gun on you in the parking lot. At that point in time it doesn't matter what he wants. If you don't act to defend yourself, you will probably die without ever knowing the "why" behind his actions and demands.

Knowing the local, state, and federal laws governing self-defense criteria is paramount to both protecting you after the act legally and to giving you confidence to act within the law during the act. That means you're going to need a more practical understanding, one that is less oriented on understanding or "curing" the criminal and more on stopping him.

Force Decided

Unfortunately for you as the victim in this case, the attacker has predetermined what he is willing to do to obtain what he wants from you. Your disadvantage is that you don't know the extent of what that willingness is. Case in point, you might be getting mugged and through your compliance you get shot. From your perspective, you were doing what he wanted—

you were complying—and you still got shot! Why? Because somewhere in that demented little brain of his, he still saw you as a threat that needed to be eliminated. I call it "comply and die." You can never assume that through compliance you will be unharmed.

Resistance

Predators have a sharp instinct. One way for an unarmed victim to survive such an attack is to "get crazy" on the attacker. Fight fire with fire by unleashing your "animal within." Fight back and do so with the utmost ferocity. Use the most brutal fighting options you have available, such as blinding him using your fingers to push his eyes into his head or crippling him with kicks or elbows. Then…escape! This may sound "crazy," but what other options do you have?

Predators typically won't mess with you if they think you're crazier than they are.

Types of Violent Attacks

This list is not all inclusive. I am including it to give you an understanding of what criminals want and how they might go about getting it. Remember what we have discussed earlier in this chapter and see if your demeanor, posture, and awareness could see it coming, and more importantly, think about your level of "craziness." See if you have enough craziness to not become a victim.

Gang Initiation
- violent acts to obtain membership
- typically are random in nature
- use of multiple attackers

Drug Seekers
- unorthodox approaches
- no plan
- no limit on physical violence, though it usually escalates
- start slow, but gets angry quickly

Robbers
- typically uses intimidation first through a show of force
- speed is paramount
- planned to some degree
- set goal in mind
- often willing to kill

Carjackers
- could be using it to get away from a previously committed crime
- urgency
- takes by surprise
- violent and angry
- speed is paramount
- you could be a hostage

Rapist
- mentally unstable
- needs to be in control
- you probably know him
- thinks you won't resist
- may use drugs to subdue victim
- victims can be murdered even after complying
- sodomized
- takes pleasure in your pain
- violent control during sex is often a turn on

Home Invader

- planned to some degree
- knows you might be home
- might not stop at just physical assets
- collateral damage might make you compliant
- could be multiple assailants involved

A Note from EJ...

Understanding your enemy gives you more information with which you can make a better decision.

Criminals do not die by the hands of the law. They die by the hands of other men.

—George Bernard Shaw

5

Heads Up

There are numerous burglaries and assaults that could have been prevented entirely. Unfortunately, most people tend to subscribe to the notion that "crime won't happen to me." Regrettably, criminals thrive on unsuspecting, unprotected, and unprepared individuals. A complacent mindset is a criminal's number-one turn on.

Criminals are predators! They prey on those they perceive to be weak. It does not matter if you don't feel weak. If a criminal perceives you as weak, they will pounce! Let me be clear that when I refer to "weak," it has nothing to do with your physical or mental prowess, but everything to do with your lack of situational awareness and preparation.

Situational Awareness

Situational awareness simply means being wholly, thoroughly aware of everything going on around you. This is true whether you are at home, at work, at the mall, at school, in a restaurant, driving, traveling, out for a walk or run, out with the guys or the girls…well, you get the point—anywhere! You must know who is near you and what is going on all around at all times. Primarily, the criminal seeks out individuals who appear to be in "la la land" and unaware that they are a few feet away from them and ready to attack.

Situational Preparation

Situational Preparedness is a result of understanding what vulnerabilities you, your family, and your home possess that a potential criminal would attempt to exploit. Conducting a comprehensive "Threat Assessment" of your current personal and residential security is the key to identifying the security flaws in your everyday life. These flaws increase your susceptibility to becoming the victim of criminal activity. This analysis should be completed as soon as possible and performed by a professional.

It is not enough to lock your doors at night. It is not enough to own a German Shepherd or any other "large and scary" four-legged creature. It is not enough to just carry pepper spray. You must know who the criminal is likely to target for their next crime. You must know what the criminal is looking for in a potential victim. You must know where the criminal is likely to conduct his next attack. You must know when the criminal is going to strike. And, finally, you must know why the criminal is committing this violent act. Remember, criminals are predators and they attack those they perceive to be weak.

A Note from EJ…

Take a look from the outside in. Could a criminal perceive you as weak?

Weak = "unaware," "unprepared," "complacent," "unbelieving"

Crime is a pandemic that is fast taking over the world. With the recession in the world's economy, fraud, corruption, theft, falsehood, and violent crime is rampant. In realizing that hurt people hurt others, one should understand that the chance of one becoming a victim of crime is no longer a mere possibility, but a reality. The purpose of this book is to advise you on how to close up some of the loopholes in your private life that may enable potential criminals the opportunity to penetrate.

Remember, a fort with weak cornerstones will quickly fall. A castle built on sand will come crumbling down in a short time. Naivety for you should be a thing of the past and you should rather be acquiring skills in self-protection and strategic living, and you should be seeking wisdom above all else. It is not the intent of this chapter to raise your fear level, but to rather serve as a practical preventative survival methodology.

Survival Methodology

Keep a proper view on life

As we go about our daily lives, you and I are constantly evaluating and re-evaluating. Sometimes we elevate one thing over another. Sadly, the thing we just elevated was of no real importance, but we just made that unimportant thing the most important thing in our lives. The unimportant thing at that moment could be money, a relationship, an asset, a job, or a person, yet we elevated it by our own choice.

Conduct a priority check on a regular basis to ensure you have life in perspective and that nothing that you value has become out of sync in relation to the rest of life. Failure to do this could place you at a risk of becoming a victim of crime. Potential criminals often study their victims and view areas where the victim is highly emotionally invested as a possible weak link for penetration.

Protect yourself

Vulnerability is beneficial as it keeps you connected with your "humanness." In our current society, vulnerability should be run through a sounding board of wisdom before being expressed. The reasons for this suggestion ties in with the point mentioned above.

Watch the company you keep

It has been said, "Bad company corrupts good character." This is true. People also judge us on the company we keep. Often, however, the seemingly most innocent person can turn out to be the most vicious at heart when provoked. This is, therefore, not a foolproof methodology. I can tell you from experience, however, that keeping a small circle of close friends whose actions and lifestyle you have observed in a variety of circumstances is wise. Exposing yourself to a large community of people without applying good judgment is foolish.

Keep strangers out of your home

Due to the economy, "living with a buddy" is becoming a more common trend. Bachelor apartments are now housing several "buddies" because of the shared expenses and the relatively cheaper living costs while sacrificing space. Families are even fast reducing their living space. The reason for mentioning this is that you or your "buddies" can easily invite a vicious criminal into your home or onto your property without being aware of it. Don't pick up strangers and invite them into your home. Don't easily go home with strangers either.

Home security

This depends on the area you live in. Some areas are more prone to crime than others and therefore this needs to be placed into perspective. Comply with your insurance companies' minimum-security requirements.

Insurance companies have a large database of losses per area that are made available to them. The better companies make security suggestions to their clients based on loss history specific to the area they reside in. Although not foolproof, precautionary measures are recommended for a reason. Try to have a little more security installed than your neighbors. The reason for this additional security may make your neighbors' houses more attractive to an opportunist thief or armed robber at crunch time.

Be cautious with dangerous objects in your home

Because a vicious murder can be committed with an item like a garden spade, one should be careful and responsible when it comes to your living environment. Keep dangerous objects, like firearms, safely locked away according to the laws of your state when not in use.

Don't leave your valuables out

Keep valuables, like expensive jewelry, cash, and passports, under lock and key when not in use.

Be skeptical of your home assistants

Some families have maids, home care assistants for the ill or elderly, gardeners, in-home childcare providers, and perhaps music teachers that come and go from the house. Use a reputable agency to locate such assistants. If you hire directly, take the time and make the small investment necessary to check credentials and references. Many thefts and armed robberies, once investigated, point straight to the home assistant.

Neighborhood watch

Some communities have neighborhood watches or resort to protecting their communities by gating off certain residential streets and appointing a guard to man an entrance point for these areas. All these things are not foolproof, but serve as deterrents. Thieves would, more often than not, rather bother the suburb next door that doesn't have these little inconveniences.

Don't walk alone at night or in potentially unsafe areas

In some communities, this is still safe, but in most, this is viewed as a high risk and caution should be exercised. There is an element of safety in numbers and to deny this is foolishness.

Break routine as much as possible

Suspecting criminals watch for a routine in a potential victim's lifestyle. The more information they have about the victim, the better. Try to not arrive at home or leave for work at exactly the same time every day. Control freaks who live by strict agendas, time frames, and routines are at risk of being victims of crime. Being overly controlling of your environment is not going to protect you from this possible risk. Everything in balance is the key.

Build a reputation of integrity

Ensure you keep your life clean and pure at all times. Live above reproach. This way, nobody will be able to blackmail you, be successful in bribing you to protect information, or correctly point fingers of blame at you. Guard your heart and your reputation. Teach your children to do the same. Your family deserves this.

Be aware of snatch-and-grab opportunities

The basics like holding tightly on to your handbag in public places, being aware of potential pickpockets, not flashing cash in public, or not leaving your cell phone or purse on the car seat next to you or in public view while driving always apply.

A Note from EJ...

While you can't possibly prevent all crime from happening, you can reduce your exposure. Criminals search for possible victims. I don't want to discount random crime from the equation, but in reality you can't predict nor plan for "random." Being at the right place at the wrong time might happen. When it does though, you have to make some very serious and potentially life-altering decisions. Awareness is key. Being aware of your situation and mentally prepared for a fight gives you the highest chance for survival.

The successful warrior is the average
man, with laser-like focus.

—Bruce Lee

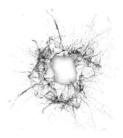

6

Mindset

To establish the ideal mindset for thwarting a violent criminal, you must first understand how we compute information under stress. One of the best ideologies used today is the OODA Loop created by John Boyd. This "loop" of intellectual computation reveals some interesting systematic responses we naturally endure in order to come to the "action" phase of our response.

If we understand how we go about computing provided or perceived information and the nuances of each step of the four steps, then we can train ourselves to move quickly from one stage to another, again, to get us to the action phase. When dealing with a violent criminal hell bent on doing you harm, you have only seconds to make a decision. Understanding how we make decisions allows us to reduce the actual time it takes to make the decision, thus getting into the fight or away from the fight sooner. Time is life! The more time we take to act the more disadvantaged we are.

OODA Loop

US Air Force Colonel John Boyd was arguably one of the most important American military thinkers in the twentieth century. He is best known for his formulation of the "OODA Loop" (also known as OODA cycle or Boyd's loop) as a model for competitive decision making. It is a concept that has been strategically applied at individual as well as group levels. Understanding the OODA loop allows you to prepare general tactics for commonly encountered situations as well as specific tactics when detailed circumstances are known ahead of time.

Colonel Boyd also left his mark on air combat tactics, maneuver warfare, and what we now call "fourth-generation warfare." On no branch of the service was his influence greater than on the US Marine Corps. "From John Boyd," wrote General Charles Krulak, then the Marine commander, "we learned about competitive decision making on the battlefield—compressing time, using time as an ally."

An aggressive man, Boyd naturally favored the offense, as exemplified by the blitzkrieg or "lightning war" advocated by the Chinese master Sun-Tzu, and the British partisan leader T. E. Lawrence, better known as Lawrence of Arabia. Boyd died in 1997. He left us with the model for competitive decision-making called the OODA Loop.

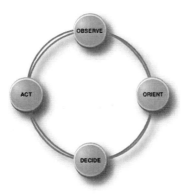

Figure 1: OODA Loop Diagram

O—Observe
O—Orient
D—Decide
A—Act

The OODA Loop shows that you first have to get information (Observe). Once you have the information, you now determine what it means to you and what you can do about it (Orient). With that, you can make your decision (Decide), based on your observations and orientation, and take action (Act) appropriately. Conversely, the actions necessary resulting from the "Decide phase" for your opponent can be altered by affecting the information the opponent receives and how he applies that information when orienting upon it.

Writer Robert Greene wrote in an article called "OODA and You," that the proper mindset, "internet," is to let go a little, to allow some of the chaos to become part of your mental system, and to use it to your advantage by simply creating more chaos and confusion for the opponent. You funnel the inevitable chaos of the assault back in the direction of the attacker. An entity (whether an individual or an organization) that can process this cycle quickly, observing and reacting to unfolding events more rapidly than an opponent, can thereby "get inside" the opponent's decision cycle and gain the advantage.

Concept

When performing the OODA Loop process (Figure 1) you observe the situation, orient yourself, decide what to do, and then do it. Then the process repeats itself.

- Observe means to know what is happening through any of your five senses, not just sight.
- Orient means to understand the meaning of what you observed.
- Decide is weighing the options available and picking one.
- Act is carrying out the decision.

Reactionary Gap

Simply put, the reactionary gap is the distance between two individuals in which an action can be rendered. Here is an example. If two people are standing a foot apart facing each other, the first one is given instructions to touch the second one as fast as he can while the second one is told to slap the first person's hand away before he gets touched. The second person will never succeed because he has to go through the full OODA loop before he can react, and by that time, the first person will have already touched him. If the two people move farther apart, the second person is more likely to have enough time to react because the greater distance gives him enough time to observe and orient himself to the threat. The greater distance also adds time to implement the action. Because the second person already knows what the first person is going to do and has made a decision on how he will react, the second person now moves instantly from observe to act.

Application for Ground Fighting

Your opponent's OODA loop can be broken in a ground fight by simply changing tactics before he can get to the act portion of the loop. If I had an opponent in some sort of joint lock or choke who finally started making headway against my hold, I would quickly switch tactics and attack another limb. He would start all over again and attempt to break this new hold. Before he could make much headway, I would switch again and get him in a different choke. The entire time we were on the ground fighting, he was expending most of the energy. That was because I was always ahead of him in the OODA cycle switching tactics before he could respond effectively. The entire time I was using little effort and great technique while he was getting fatigued fighting against my attacks. His fatigue made my control of the OODA loop even stronger.

Application for SWAT team entries

The SWAT team makes entry on a room by throwing a flashbang. A flashbang is a nonlethal explosive device used to temporarily disorient an enemy's senses. It is designed to produce a blinding flash of light and loud noise without causing permanent injury. It goes off disorienting the occupants and temporarily blinding them with the flash. While the occupants are disoriented by the light and concussion, the team enters and engages the suspects before they can react. The orient phase of the OODA loop is broken and, until the suspect can regain his sight and a slight sense of hearing, can't move on to the decide and act phase, thus rendered incapacitated.

Application for you

In each of these examples, action beats reaction. Yet we often have to react to circumstances and people around us. The trick is to use our knowledge of the OODA loop to take the offense away from our opponent. Generally that means overtaking him in the cycle by being faster or slowing him down. All of this should occur in a fraction of a second. You will repeat this thought process with every action you take and with the opponent's reaction to what you are doing.

In most deadly encounters, we are already behind in this process when the fight starts. The bad guy has already gone through his OODA Loop and is acting while you are observing. In order to regain the advantage, you must process the threat quickly and act. That forces him back to the observe phase. To illustrate, consider the following scenario:

At a gas station you are filling up your vehicle with gas, the occupant of the vehicle suddenly opens his door and gets out with a gun in his hand. Bad Guy = Act, You = Observe. At this initial phase of the battle, the bad guy has the advantage. He has already gone through his OODA Loop and is about to shoot you dead.

You, on the other hand, are caught flatfooted. You are filling up your vehicle with gas, probably in an area where you have no cover. How do you regain the advantage? You quickly sidestep as you draw your weapon and are no longer standing where the suspect thought you would be. You = Act, Bad Guy = Observe. Just this simple movement can make the bad guy go through his OODA Loop again while you are laying accurate fire on him. In a gunfight, these small shifts often determine who lives and who dies.

The above scenario is simplified, but it does show how the process works. While your mind will have to go through the entire loop with each new piece of information that is presented, the bottom line is this—the faster you can go from "Observe" to "Act," the more advantage you will have.

In order to make this transition quickly, it requires training. There are many ways to train your body and mind for this. Sparring, force-on-force, and scenario training are a few examples.

When getting to formal training is not possible, another way to train is to visualize various scenarios that may occur in your particular environments—in your home, your office building, your office, your car, your boat, on your bike. As you visualize a particular environment, develop a course of action. Ask yourself, "What will I do if a predator and I meet in (name the place)?" Visualizing a situation like seeing yourself walk into your office and meeting a predator, orienting yourself in that situation (noting egress areas, distances, lighting, furniture, etc.), and deciding how you will react—"If he does this, I would do that?"—is an effective technique for training your thinking to move quickly through your OODA Loop. When you perform multiple visualizations, you become oriented and decided. Doing so allows you to move directly from "Observe" to "Act."

Visualization training has been used for many years by athletes and has proven very beneficial. Of the utmost importance in visualization training is that you maintain situational awareness. If you are not aware of your surroundings, you will not properly assess the threat and will be doomed to failure. This brings us to the Cooper's Color Code of Awareness.

Col. Cooper'sColor Code of Awareness

The Color Code of Awareness was developed by Colonel Jeff Cooper, USMC (1920–2008). Colonel Cooper was a combat veteran and a businessman. He was one of the most prolific firearms trainers and theorists of the modern age. He founded the American Pistol Institute in 1976 and authored many books and articles relating to gunfighting. The color code has been modified over the years by various trainers and schools and even the federal government, which uses the color code model to indicate "force protection" or threat levels. You might have noticed a colored indicator on a government building. If so, you have been introduced to Cooper's Color Code of Awareness as modified by the federal government. I will focus on Colonel Cooper's original model.

| Unaware and Unprepared | Relaxed but Alert | Specific Alert | Fight Trigger |

Figure 2 – Col. Cooper's Color Code of Awareness Diagram

The Color Code of Awareness scale has nothing to do with tactical situations. It does not represent a physical alertness level, but instead it indicates your state of mind as it relates to possible or potential threats. Cooper broke the amount of mental attention at any given moment into different levels. Each level is identified by a particular color. The lowest level of alertness is indicated by white. The highest level of alertness is indicated by red.

White—"Oh my God! I can't believe this is happening!"

In this mental state you are totally relaxed, not paying attention to your surroundings, and not prepared to defend against a threat.

Yellow—"I might have to defend myself today."

In this mental state, you are relaxed, but alert in your surroundings for possible threats. This is the condition you should be in throughout your day.

Orange—"I might have to shoot someone sooner than later."

In this mental state, you have identified a potential threat and are focused on it with your mental trigger set. "If that person does X, I will need to stop them." Your weapon usually remains holstered. If the threat proves to be nothing, you return to the yellow mental state.

Red—"If X happens, I will shoot that person. X happens and the fight is on!"

This mental state indicates that your "fight trigger" is when you are actually in the fight.

A Note from EJ...

Applying the Color Code of Awareness should become a daily occurrence for you. Think about it throughout the day and evaluate what condition you find yourself in. Condition Yellow is where you should be most of the time. If you drift into condition White, you are putting yourself at risk. When you catch yourself there, wake up and get back to Yellow. Study the OODA Loop and Color Code of Awareness. Incorporate it into your daily activities. When the moment of truth comes, and you decisively win your deadly encounter, you'll be glad you did!

I must study politics and war that my sons may have liberty to study mathematics and philosophy.

—John Adams

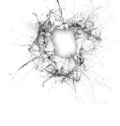

7

Science of Gunfighting

Gunfight! The fictional version of what our mind's eye quickly conjures up when we hear the word "gunfight" comes from what movies and television would like us to believe. That a "gunfight" is simply two Old West gunfighters squaring off with each other on a dusty street. This over-romanticized image of the gunfight was born in the dime novels of the late nineteenth century and perpetuated in the film era. In actuality, the "real" gunfights of the Old West were rarely that civilized.

In fact, there are several inaccuracies about these "romanticized" gunfights, the first being that very rarely did the gunfighters actually "plan" for a gunfight to occur. The second is the "calling out" of their enemy for dueling action in the street. Instead, most of these many fights took place in the heat of the moment when tempers flared, and more often than not, with the aid of a little "dark bottle" courage. They also didn't occur at a distance of fifteen paces, with each gunfighter taking one shot, one falling dead to the ground, and the other standing as a "hero" before a dozen gathered onlookers.

Instead, these fights were usually close up and personal, with a number of shots blasted from their "six shooters," often resulting in innocent bystanders being hit by a stray bullet. For many of the fights, it would be difficult to tell who had even won, until the black power smoke cleared. It is especially important to note that the gunfights then—and now—are rarely planned.

Today's modern gunfight in a combat zone is either the result of an ambush or a raid. The ambush, being the most common of the two, causes soldiers to react by devising a counter-ambush plan then implementing it. Luckily for our soldiers they have left the FOB (forward operating base) following the first and second rules for gunfighting: 1, Bring a gun, and, 2, Bring friends with guns!

Modern day gunfighting and its history continue to be studied heavily. Many commit their lives to perfecting their gunfighting skills and tactics. More importantly, they commit their mindset in much the same way as a samurai warrior committed his mindset, allowing that mindset to take over their body's actions and reactions.

All too often, we, as Second Amendment-expressing gun carriers, go about preparing for our deadly encounter by continuing to go to a static range and punch as small a hole as we can into paper targets. Our mindset being that we will knowingly square off to a front facing threat and victoriously defeat him with our superior shooting skills then turn to the beautiful woman we have just saved, give her a head nod, and say, "Are you all right?" We are guilty of consistently training on the aspects of shooting we are naturally good at. The strong-handed weaver or isosceles stance is the common picture of the guy next to you, and more than likely, you too! While that is a good start for the beginner, the true warrior has to be ready for the unknown fight that will be brought to bear. To do that you must break out of your comfort zone and train in those things that we are not good at. We must train our mind to see things we might not see if we are not looking for them. We must perceive the fighting space, move in it ruthlessly, and dominate the fight.

To understand the dynamics of a gunfight, you need to expand your education up a little farther than just the trigger pulling. When thinking about modern day gunfighting or handling threats of any kinds, there are four factors I want you to consider. I want you to integrate them into your thinking so that when you are studying, while you are training, and simply when you are out and about, these principles are second nature to you. Once you understand the Science of Gunfighting, then your training, and ultimately your fighting, will take on a whole new meaning.

Threat Vector

First there is the threat vector. The threat vector is the line of approach the threat is taking directly to you. Whether it is a physical attacker, a knife, or even a bullet, the path that is the most direct line to you is the threat vector. It could come from any direction too, not just the two scenarios you have played over and over in your head. The threat vector sets up the reaction and action requirements and helps define the next factors.

Space

Second is space. Space is the immediate area in which you must deal with the threat. To help define the space, start by asking yourself these questions:

- What is around me?
- Where can I go?
- Where can he go?
- How close am I to the threat?
- Is there anything in the space that I can use to tilt the advantage in my favor?

Use these questions to establish where you are so you can figure out how not to be there for the punch to land, the knife to cut, or the bullet to hit.

Time

The third factor is that of time. Time in a gunfight, particularly, is dictated by space and threat vector, and not by your physical ability to draw or move off the line of attack. Ask yourself:

- Can I run away?
- Can I get to my weapon in time to defend myself?
- Do I have time to secure my kids or do I have to act now?

Force

The last factor is force. Force is defined as the immediate threat brought to bear by the attacker. In a physical attack, such as a hand-to-hand fight, using your opponent's force against him is always superior to overpowering him. There are issues to trying to overpower someone. It is possible that in your effort to overpower your opponent, you could apply too much power, causing unnecessary injury to him, landing yourself in costly (and perhaps embarrassing) legal trouble. In court, the idea of "appropriate force" to neutralize the threat is applied. Your counterattack should be equal, in the eyes of the court, to that brought on you. Remember, the bad guy sets the time, place, and force applied much like the ambushes out troops face.

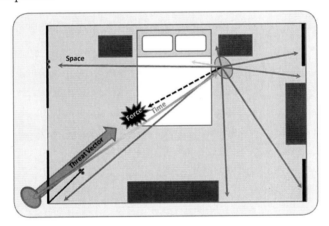

Did you recognize the threat, process it, control your reaction and begin to act before he has closed the distance on the threat vector?

Our "scenarios" are just that, thoughts of possible situations that could have no bearing on the reality of the current situation. That's why we train for everything. Even as silly as it sounds, you never know when or where your encounter will happen.

As with hand-to-hand fighting, using your own body weight against an attacker grants you more options and requires less motion and body strength when dealing with them. Nearly always, this advantage keeps you in the fight longer because your fatigue sets in slower. As it relates to gunfighting, it's not who fires first, but who fires and hits first! Accurate hits end gunfights fast!

Science

So how do these factors interact with each other to make science?

Science refers to a body of knowledge itself, of the type that can be rationally explained and reliably applied. Over the course of the nineteenth century, the word *science* became increasingly associated with the scientific method itself, as a disciplined way to study the natural world, including physics, chemistry, geology, and biology. Science, through observation and experiments, helps us define principles and express theory. These expressions are then formed into knowledge. In order for us to obtain knowledge, we must look at how we obtain true knowledge through the types of learning styles.

Learning Styles

The three most common types are (in no particular order):

- Spatial: You prefer learning through pictures and images
- Linguistic: You prefer using words, both in speech and writing
- Kinesthetic: You prefer using your body, hands, and sense of touch

Most of us learn more proficiently by doing rather than reading, lecture, or viewing images. Kinesthetic learning style refers to acquiring knowledge through movement. It is the movement that allows our senses to gain the most information about the environment we are in at the time. Incorporating the use of movement in your training will reinforce the concepts discussed here. In most gunfighting classes, you will be taught, upon recognition of a threat, to "MOVE!" Get off the threat vector and gain space. If we practice recognizing these concepts then we will naturally enact them under stress. As with being a kinesthetic learner, you will instantly recognize these elements as they appear, but without the knowledge to utilize this information, we will rarely make the right decisions.

Retention vs. Comprehension

This brings us to another aspect of learning: retention versus comprehension. Retention is much like cramming the night before a test. We soak up as much information as we can to accurately regurgitate the next day then forget it a day or week later. Comprehension goes beyond retention in that it is the application of the information and, therefore, reusable regardless of the context or situation. Understanding that the majority of us are kinesthetic learners, then getting out of our chairs and "doing" it will lead to comprehension. So to put it in context, telling you to recognize that a threat is behind you and pivot on your weak side front foot to the rear, and draw, will only trigger what you are capable of mentally picturing and playing out in your mind. It is not committed to memory nor is it able to be correctly applied in a "time is life" situation when you are under stress and duress.

Conversely, if I demonstrate the series of movement to you and have you do the series over and over again through several shooting classes, the series becomes instinct, reactionary, automatic, and thereby surpassing the retention of learning. At this level, you will have the knowledge and skill to perform the series correctly and upon demand. This is because your modality of learning was utilized to seal it into your comprehension. It also explains why attending only one or two shooting classes may not prepare you for a gunfight despite what some instructors will tell you.

Okay! Enough with the professor speak; let's get down to the application!

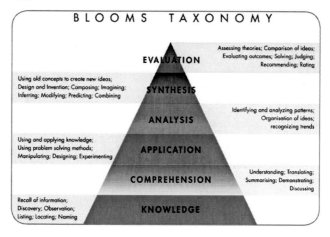

Application

In any situation, recognition of the threat and its vector happens first. With it, your mind has established the type of threat. As stated earlier, you will never know which direction the threat will appear until it is ready to be discovered so this puts us on the defensive. Working out of the defense puts us reacting. When we train, say for instance with our back to the threat, we are preparing our instincts to use the knowledge we gained through kinesthetic learning to properly react accordingly. This gives us the advantage of managing our space and time better.

Now that the threat and its vector have been established, we must compute the relative space we have to operate in. Space encompasses, not only distance between you and the threat, but also your area of movement away from the threat. If we are in our home and a window was just broken, we must determine how to react. This determination is eating up our precious time so understanding space is critical. If you have watched the spy movies like the Jason Bourne types, you will often see our hero entering into a restaurant or other type of establishment and noting the entrances, exits, and types of obstacles. Well, this is really done by our OGA (other government agencies) operatives during real world missions.

They are determining their "space," as well as playing the mental gymnastics on possible avenues of attack.

We can do this in our own home! We can look at how our bedroom or safe room is laid out and the possible movement options we have. We can look at how we can manipulate this space to tilt the fight to our advantage. Is there a chest of drawers we can throw down in front of our door, thus slowing the predator's entrance into the room? Is there a window we can escape out of? And the list goes on. Most times when you hear of a home invasion the victim cowers in a closet "hoping" not to be found. Maybe that was their only option, but if we understand our space we can give ourselves a greater fighting chance.

Time is key! Time for us means that we can, in fact, devise a plan. However, we didn't set the time for this event, he did, so we must manage it ruthlessly. Based on our threat recognition and its vector, we can decide what we have time to do in our given space. When we train we occasionally use shot timers to help us gauge our overall speed and proficiency on a particular drill. We can use this to elevate stress and push us to perform at a higher level than we thought possible. Well, certainly there won't be a physical shot timer in your space but effectively hitting your threat before he hits you is winning in any book. If you have time and the capacity to leave then do it. If not, get to doing what it is you're going to do!

With this information, you can now determine the force you need to apply in the vector, time, and space you estimate in order to deter, deflect, or defeat the threat. Remember, in a gunfight, the first rule is "Bring a Gun!" If you left it in your car or resting comfortably in the safe, it does you no good. As the situation unfolds and you need to skin that smoke wagon of yours out, you will undoubtedly want to use the first three factors discussed here. All your training, or lack thereof, will culminate in the blink on an eye. Most people involved in a gunfight say that time slowed down and everything seemed surreal. That is because our minds are processing the events at a higher rate than we can react to. Training under stress increases our potential for correct actions within the appropriate timetable with favorable results.

The "science of gunfighting" occurs when these four concepts come together with the physical actions of your body. Your mind will only tell your body what to do if you have trained for it…everything else is panic! Hopefully, you now have a better understanding of why we are so successful in engaging our enemies abroad. The military uses these concepts starting on day one of entry and continues to delve deeper in the science of gunfighting in order to bring perfection to the battlefield. Perfection in a gunfight is the attacker dying for his cause and you eating breakfast the next morning.

While science is used to define actions, knowledge aids us in defining what our reactions will be, and thus converting instinct into action. Animals use instinct. They don't know, nor understand, why they are doing particular actions, they just do them. Not always is their "doing" the right thing to do. We as humans have a deep intellectual understanding of ourselves and our environment and can use this knowledge to make better decisions. Utilizing these concepts, while training with vigor, gives us the advantage in a gunfight. While science may seem complicated, this is not. The best way not get punched, slashed, or shot is simply DON'T BE THERE!

Don't be there…move off the vector!
Don't be there…gain or take away space before
your attacker does!
Don't be there…recognize time and respond
accordingly!
And if you are there…apply force appropriately.

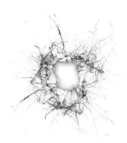

8

The Fight

The scariest time in your life will be when you have to defend your existence on this planet in a violent encounter. Your adrenaline will spike to a level you have never experienced before. Your eyes will widen to the point of breaking the connective tissue holding them into your eye sockets and your nostrils will not be able to flare enough to suck the amount of oxygen your lungs will be demanding. Your stomach will close off and you might even lose control of your bowels. Lactic acid will build rapidly in your muscles, tightening your every move while your feet will feel as if you are wearing concrete boots. This will be physically happening at the same time your mind is processing information and devising a plan for survival. There will be a mix of autonomic nervous systems reactions fighting with conscious panic. It just got real!

The short of it is—figure it out quickly and get moving! You will have to rely on your current physical stamina, past experiences, training, and a small amount of luck to survive. Everything that you are capable of doing has just culminated in this one event, and you have to execute your actions timely and accurately. I can't stress enough that this will happen fast! It will be on you in seconds and you will have even less time to act.

Up until now you might have had some training awhile back and maybe even war-gamed it in your head that ultimately ends with you victorious. Well, this is reality, and I'm quite sure that in your "war gaming," there wasn't this rush of physical and mental responses clouding your decisions and hindering your movements. As you go through the OODA Loop process, you are hit like a MAC truck with information and physical responses that are all competing for your decisions.

In a real life situation, you will not "rise" to the occasion, you will default to the highest level of training you have mastered! Let me say that again—mastered. Everything else you will do will be out of panic. In panic, you have no conscious control over your actions. You are in stimulus overload and your body's natural reaction will be fight or flight. In flight mode, hopefully, you will realize that you are trying to move away from the threat. Under the fight response, you might charge indiscriminately toward the threat without a plan for victory. Both can get you killed. Without training your intuitive responses, you are relying on the "luck" factor. Luck, sadly, doesn't choose a side in a fight.

In most deadly encounters, one side gains the advantage of surprise then compels the other side into compliance through the perceived disparity of their situation. This disparity comes from the situation failing to present a clear way out, thus making it futile to resist. He has won! You are left with no choice (because this is how you perceive the situation) but to comply and die.

There is no worse feeling than that of forced disparity. It is the feeling of complete brokenness. I liken it to the African water buffalo being attacked by a pack of hungry lions. They have it by the neck. The water buffalo is not dead yet, but it also cannot escape. Realizing this, he chooses to fall to the ground and accept his fate...before he dies. The water buffalo has fought as much as he could. In the end, he could not see a way out. It is a slow death as the lions start eating at his body before he is dead. He fought as much as he could but in the end could not see a way out, so he chooses to lie down and be devoured.

Intuitive responses

We as humans are intellectually superior to any other animal on this planet. Because of our intellectual superiority, we are also more unpredictable. We have within us the means to resist surprise attacks because we have studied the natural responses, and unlike the animal kingdom, we have the ability to pass this information to others through personal interactions, books, television, and other media formats. If we use this information to build strong, intuitive responses through training, then we minimize our innate response. This then moves our actions from reaction to action. The ability to move quickly using solid foundational intuitive actions will assist us in survival.

You have heard the saying "Don't think. Just do." Well, the military has taken this to the next level by preconditioning through training the "do" to be what we know to be the right response, eliminating the need for conscious thought. It's merely the act of training the intuitive responses to be the correct responses. We obtain this high state of readiness by training in a dynamic and realistic environment with plausible scenarios that give us a solid foundation of experiences to help us problem solve on the fly. You may only ever be in one gunfight, but if you have trained on a thousand different dynamic and realistic gunfighting scenarios, you are more apt to engage the enemy quicker and with more violence, thus defeating him. As I have discussed earlier in this book, the need to process information quickly and accurately is paramount. We must utilize existing proven methods to aid us in getting to the act portion of the decision making process. Once we act, our skills and abilities (honed through training) take center stage.

You can't do anything about the bullet with your name on it, but you can do something about the ones addressed "To Whom It May Concern"!

Survival

In a gunfight, you have two primary issues—your life and everything else. Your survival is of the utmost concern, because if you don't survive you can't help anyone else. Too often, when I talk to women about carrying everyday, I am told that they would not protect themselves, but they would die for their children. My response is a visceral reaction that conveys my disgust for this mentality. I ask them if they want their children growing up in some crappy foster home and being raised by some old hag they don't even know, to which they angrily respond "No!" Then, don't die! Fight! The thought that mothers would protect their children but not themselves is asinine. Look, you have to survive in order to protect others…it's that simple!

The mindset is that of ruthless survival, not immortality.

—EJ Owens, Legally Concealed

Upon recognition of a threat, we orient ourselves and begin the decision-making process. Here is where realistic training plays a key component to your survival. What do you do? Move! Move from where you are and then keep moving. I don't care if it is to cover at this point, the key is to move.

During training, I have my students move during the draw so as to break the attackers OODA Loop. Now this is where we start multitasking. You are moving off the line of the attacker's threat vector and utilizing the given space to gain a tactical advantage. By moving, you are making it harder for the attacker to hit you with the bullet, fist, stick, etc. Speed is important but not as important as the movement itself. Once you have started your movement you must incorporate your next action, which is to either counter his violence or exit the battle space. Either way, get to doing it, and do it quickly.

If you are going to return fire, then get your gun up and direct it toward him immediately. At intimate distances of five feet or less, simply pointing your gun center mass on his chest and pulling the trigger will do the job. There is no need to squint your nondominant eye to align your sights. Sight picture is accomplished by bringing the barrel of your gun in line with your nose. Press out and center the gun with the line your nose extending directly in front of you. At five feet or less, this is sufficient to neutralize the attacker. Your training will help you get on target faster.

The faster we kill them the less they will shoot at us.

When faced with a real deadly threat, someone untrained or undertrained most likely will hesitate, probably costing that person his or her life. The untrained or undertrained might fumble when getting his or her gun out of the holster because their draw technique wasn't practiced enough, costing the person to sustain an injury, if not his or her life. Maybe the person will crank off a round negligently, hitting an innocent bystander because of the mind racing and adrenaline rush that was not expected due to a lack of training. Realistic training will develop solid intuitive shooting stance and draw techniques. With proper repetition, you will recognize the threat, control your mindset and breathing, draw your weapon, and take the kill shot with ease and proficiency.

Wyatt Protocol

After moving off line of the threat vector and deciding to draw your gun, it is time to get accurate shots on target and then start heading for cover. I follow and teach the Wyatt protocol (FAST) for gunfighting. It says to…

Fight
Fight, Fight, FIGHT!

Assess
Do I need to fight anymore?

Scan
Do I need to fight anyone else?

Top Off
Prepare to fight again.

Once the initial fighting is over, you need to determine if the immediate threat is neutralized. You do this by looking around for any other threats that might need to be fought. FBI statistics say that you have over a 50 percent chance of being attacked by multiple attackers. If so, start fighting them *now*! Once you have determined that there are no more threats and are in a position of cover, reload your gun and get ready for the next fight.

Accurate shots

Legally and morally, we are responsible for all stray rounds. For legal and tactical reasons, we want to stop the attacker with as few shots as possible. Let's define accurate shots. Accurate shots are those shots that hit either of the two areas vital to life—the brain and the heart.

The brain is enclosed in the skull. The skull is thick bone purposely developed by the body in order to protect this extremely fragile organ. In order to penetrate the brain and stop the attacker, we must place the shots in the cranial ocular cavity that lies behind the eyes and nose. This means that you should aim for the nose. Unless you train often, your body's natural instinct will be to have you hand "kick" (or go up) with the gun as it forces the bullet out of its barrel. If you aim for the eyes and then the gun "goes up," the shot may only glance the attacker's head. Shots may also skip off an attacker's skull due to the convex nature of its shape and bone density. So aim for the nose.

The human heart is about the size of a closed fist— that is, five to six inches across depending on the angle of measurement. The aim point for the heart is high in the chest and center of the nipple line. The spongy bone over the center of your chest is your sternum. It is strong enough to hold your rib cage intact but can also flex to take a blow without cracking. It will not stop a bullet!

You want to ensure that the attacker starts loosing blood. This means that their blood pressure will drop and they will cease to be a threat. Shooting in the heart stops it. Once the heart stops, so does everything else.

Cover

Seeking cover is one of those things taught as a consideration in shooting schools. Because of the practicality of actually having cover on the range, we rarely integrate it into our live training regimen. We in the gun community talk about seeking cover like it's an implied task that we will naturally do. I'm here to tell you that what you do in training is the most you can expect to do in a real gunfight.

You need to put cover between you and the attacker as soon as possible. Cover is defined as anything that will stop a bullet. Cover is relative to the weapon being fired at you! It is different than concealment. Concealment is the attacker not being able to see you, but it doesn't stop a bullet. We use concealment when we are hunting deer and turkey, but if that deer or turkey could shoot back at us then we would be dead. That's a wild thought, I know, but you get my point. Once behind cover, look for target indicators like a shoe, elbow, knee, hip, hands, or maybe a shadow to indicate location and position. Here is the tip of the day:

If you can see it, you can shoot it.

However, this goes both ways. When shooting using cover, never come out of cover from the same spot twice in a row. Remember, be unpredictable in order to break the attacker's OODA Loop. Keep him observing while you are acting.

We have been shackled by "fair play" and it could get you killed!

Legal Battle

Once you have eliminated the threat and you are safe from any additional threats, the next battle is ramping up, the legal battle. I am telling you this for a reason so pay attention because it is vital to your continued walk on this planet. Holster your gun before the police arrive or drop it immediately when they get there. They will not hesitate to shoot you! The last information they received was that someone was shooting up the place and then they see you with a gun in your hands and possibly another person's blood all over you (shooting an attacker up close and personal during a struggle is a bloody mess). They are going to take you into custody. You will get a free pair of steel bracelets to wear during your taxpayer-funded taxi ride to the iron-barred Hilton. You will want to plead your case to convince the officers on the scene of your innocence, but...

Shut your mouth and ask for a lawyer!

You don't have to answer any questions. The police on the scene cannot pass judgment and declare you "not guilty," they are merely note takers of the event. The decision to press charges falls on the District Attorney (DA). He or she will be briefed on the crime scene findings and the charges that should be considered against you. The DA will then decide what the state will do to you next. In the meantime, you are alive! You survived a heinous act of attempted murder and you came out victorious. You need to understand that our legal system has a process it follows and the process progresses slowly. This will take time to play out. So yes! You were forced into a situation against your will where you had to defend your life from a violent attacker. You survived only to be forced against your will to battle our legal system for your continued freedom. Here is where you need to be at peace with your actions.

Emotional Battle

A clear conscience is of great benefit while you await your outcome. Here is where I rely on my faith to carry me. I know that he guides my path but that I must take responsibility for my own actions. You will go through the following emotions in this order:

- Denial—This can't be really happening!
- Guilt—Why did I shoot him? Maybe I shouldn't have shot him.
- Anger—Why did he make me shoot him?
- Depression—I'm a murderer and will have to live with that.

- Adjustment—I did what I had to do.
- Reconstruction—It happened and I cannot change that. I have to move on.
- Acceptance—It's part of me, but it doesn't define me.

This chapter exposes the reality of the burden we bear when carrying a gun for self-protection. It's not sexy nor is it ideal, but it is what survival demands. The acceptance of this burden is the foundation for what we accept when we strap on that burner and roll out into danger zone that is our world. If this burden is too much for you to bear, you can always be the African water buffalo and lie down and accept your fate.

We all die; I just want to die on my own terms.

—EJ Owens, Legally Concealed

The fear of death follows from the fear of life. A man who lives fully is prepared to die at any time.

—Mark Twain

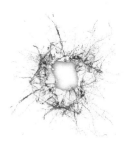

9

A Hero's Death

Death teaches us so much about life and about ourselves, even though it can be very difficult to comprehend and experience. As a culture we don't really talk about death, deal with it, or face it in an authentic way. Death often seems too scary, mysterious, personal, loaded, heavy, emotional, tragic, and more.

The thought of death can be detrimental to us in a gunfight. It can cause us to hold in a position of cover and panic, losing the advantage of movement, allowing the attacker's actions to control your OODA Loop resulting in your demise. So because of the fear of death we die without a well-fought fight. Personally, I will not, while there is still a breath left in me, allow these animals to ruthlessly murder my family or me while I stand by out of fear for my own safety. I will commit, in the moment, everything that I am to ending the threat to my family and myself. This commitment is only realized by controlling fear.

There is a fine line that separates fear from courage. Courage is action despite fear. You truly do not know how you will react in a deadly encounter because we can't replicate the amount of physiological and emotional duress that you will be under in a training environment. However, you can learn to control any emotional deviation from your training that you might experience with a clear and decisive mindset. A mindset of determination and courage will aid you greatly through "events," but the real key to survival is to live, live fully with no regrets. Commit now, this minute, before you continue to read this book that you will live your life to its fullest.

I have seen death in many of its forms. I have seen innocence die and those whom probably deserved to die slow and painfully, i.e., rapists and child molesters ("deserved" is based on my own moral and ethical code). While we have all known someone who has died, most of us separate ourselves from that experience. We just do not like to think about it. After all, it is a long way off, right? So we walk around on autopilot, caught up in the business—the busyness—of life. However, when we finally believe that we are going to die, we see things much differently. I have held those dying in my arms and watched their soul leave their body, both innocent and the deserving. I can tell you this, most of them at the point they recognized that it was their time instantly were filled with regret.

Regret is a negative cognitive/emotional state that involves blaming ourselves for a bad outcome, feeling a sense of loss or sorrow at what might have been or wishing we could undo a previous choice that we made. Over short time periods, people are more likely to regret actions taken and mistakes made, whereas over long time periods, they are more likely to regret actions not taken, such as missed opportunities for love or working too hard and not spending enough time with family.

Along with their regret is a longing for forgiveness and to forgive. People hurt us intentionally and unintentionally. While we need to correct people who have views that can be divisive and ill informed, it does not mean we need to wipe them out of consciousness. Relationships don't last long if we kill off those who have hurt us. Since relationships are what make life meaningful, we benefit most when we tolerate the idea that people we love are capable of both good and bad.

- Accept what you are able to do and not able to do.
- Accept the past without denying it or discarding it.
- Learn to forgive yourself and to forgive others.
- Do not assume that it is too late to get involved.

What if we embraced our own death and of those around us in a real, vulnerable, and genuine way? What if we lived life more aware of the fact that everyone around us, including ourselves, has a limited amount of time here on earth?

Embracing death consciously alters our experience of ourselves, others, and life in a fundamental and transformational way. It allows us to remember what truly matters and to put things in a healthy and empowering perspective. Doing this is much better for us than spending, perhaps wasting, our time worrying, complaining, and surviving the circumstances, situations, and dramas of our lives, isn't it?

The fruit of belief is action. And the benefit of learning how to die physically is to learn how to live spiritually. If faith is part of your life, express it in ways that seem appropriate to you. You may find comfort and hope in reading spiritual texts, attending religious services, or praying. Allow yourself to be around people who understand and support your religious beliefs.

When you make the commitment to carry a firearm for self-defense, you are putting the power of life and death within hand's reach. Treat that firearm with the respect it deserves, for today may be the day that death calls you and you must answer. Too often, we live in fear of death.

We should not fear death, but instead we should fear not living until death. Put first things first in your life. Remember, you can't take any of it with you in the end. We all die, and so it doesn't really matter how much you accomplish or how many possessions you accrue. What matters most is the amount of joy you spread, gratitude you exude, and love you cultivate.

> Make peace with yourself
> Make peace with your family
> Make peace with God

Live more consciously each day. Stop sleepwalking through life. Your life is something to be experienced, not coasted through. Escape your ego. Begin to see through new eyes. Begin a newfound life with friends and a newfound love with your family and within your marriage. Once you have your life in order, then you are able to commit fully in battle. Without hesitation you move, without fear you engage, and without remorse you are victorious. In this moment you don't think twice, there is no need to. You are at peace with yourself and your life. You express your feelings to those you need to, and you have your religious beliefs in order so that should you meet your death on the field of battle you are ready.

If I die then I die a free man who loved and lived a wholesome life with no regrets. Those that I leave behind should remember the many things that my life stood for and how I *lived* instead of merely existing. Each day I that I rise I live that day to the fullest. I pray that when I die, it is in the act of protecting innocence and that through my death, innocence continues to live.

Living without regret, sacrificing your life so that others may live…that is a hero's death. We can only hope that our own death will be worthy of such.

—EJ Owens

As I close this chapter, let me share with you this powerful speech that is as much about celebrating life, crossing over, and meeting your maker, as it is about facing the inevitable death of our mortal bodies with grace.

So live your life that the fear of death can never enter your heart.

Trouble no one about their religion. Respect others in their view, and demand that they respect yours.

Love your life, perfect your life, beautify all things in your life.

Seek to make your life long and its purpose in the service of your people.

Prepare a noble death song for the day when you go over the great divide.

Always give a word or a sign of salute when meeting or passing a friend, even a stranger, when in a lonely place.

Show respect to all people and grovel to none.

When you arise in the morning, give thanks for the food and for the joy of living.

If you see no reason for giving thanks, the fault lies only in yourself.

Abuse no one and no thing, for abuse turns the wise ones to fools and robs the spirit of its vision.

When it comes your time to die, be not like those whose hearts are filled with the fear of death, so that when their time comes they weep and pray for a little more time to live their lives over again in a different way.

Sing your death song and die like a hero going home.

—Tecumseh (1768–1813)
Native American leader, Shawnee

You can only fix one thing at a time…so don't try and solve everything at once.

—A Good Paramedic

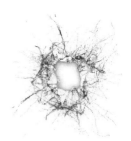

10

Bloody Hands

An intruder has entered into your home and you have grabbed your gun to defend you and your family. As you enter into the living room on your way to get the kids to safety, you meet the intruder and he is armed! You align your sights just as your youngest daughter runs to your legs screaming…the intruder fires and you fire back, hitting him square in the chest. He is down! Thankfully you are not injured, but your daughter is lying at your feet with a .380 caliber hole in her chest. The intruder missed you and hit your daughter clinging to your leg. Panic! Sheer panic! She is breathing erratically and you can see that her jugular veins are bulging out, her chest rise is uneven, and her respirations are extremely labored. What do you do?

The average response time for a metro EMS system is eight to ten minutes. In the case of a shooting, the police will have to "secure the scene" prior to the ambulance and fire truck to pull down. Now your response time is anywhere from fifteen to thirty minutes. Your daughter is probably dead by now. As a former firefighter/paramedic for a major metropolitan fire department and a trained US Army medic, I have seen this scenario too many times to count. It is just sad!

When there is shooting, somebody is going to bleed. Medical training is a must. God forbid we ever have to defend our homes, but if we do, someone will likely need it— including the attacker.

There is something you can do!

If you have first responder training and an on-hand trauma kit that is properly stocked, you can potentially save her life. I want you to understand that you are not helpless and there are skills you can learn and kit you can have to aid you in this time of need.

Training

First, go to the Red Cross website and take a CPR/First Aid course taught in your area. Getting certified in CPR/First Aid ensures that you know the basic information for helping either adults or children.

(http://www.redcross.org/takeaclass/programhighlights/cprfirstaid)

The Red Cross CPR/First Aid course provides basic instruction in CPR and wound care. This is the source for your entry into treating life-threatening injuries. They offer both certified and noncertified training options. Getting certified in CPR/First Aid and having that certification card in your wallet, however, increases your confidence that you know the basic information for helping either adults or children.

After that, look into getting additional training in emergency medical care. There are companies that offer classes that expand your learning gained in the Red Cross course. The additional training goes deeper into treating trauma, especially airway management for gunshot wounds and stabbings. There are other companies out there that provide "on the ground" immediate medical training and I don't want to exclude them so get the training where you can and as soon as you can! Also, any well-respected tactical shooting class you take should cover trauma treatment to some degree, offering you some practical experience to relate to when attending.

Trauma Kit

A properly stocked, well-placed trauma kit can mean the difference in life or death. There is rarely a situation where just one person is injured, so consider putting together several trauma kits. Keep one in your car at all times. Also, keep one upstairs and downstairs, one in the garage, and consider keeping one at your office. You should always have one in your range bag! You need to keep them, at a minimum, in these locations because they are probable locations for a conflict and also they are easier to direct someone to retrieve them for you. A trauma kit should include (at a minimum):

1 each	8" x 12" Compression Dressing
1 each	TK4 tourniquet (or SOFTT)
1 each	Gauze bandage roll
1 each	Nasopharyngeal Airway (30fr) Robertazzi Style
1 each	Surgilube® Jelly, sterile
2 each	Alcohol Prep Pad
2 each	Safety pin
1 each	Roll of duct tape
1 each	Pair of Nitrile gloves

Optional:

1 each	14ga 3.25" needle/angiocath
1 each	Chemlite® (red)
1 each	Chemlite® (green)
1 each	Ambu® Bag
1 each	Quickclot®

You can get these materials and others at these websites;

www.theemsstore.com

www.amazon.com

www.shop.darkangelmedical.com

www.tacticalresponsegear.com

Figure 3–V.O.K. from Tactical Response Gear

Treatment

There are three areas of treatments that you need to become confident in handling. Let's discuss them.

Bleeding (Hemorrhage)

Bleeding must be brought under control quickly because the victim has no way of replacing what is being lost. Bright red blood carries oxygen to our lungs and thus gives us life. Dark red blood carries deoxygenated blood back to the heart to get oxygenated again. Bright red blood and dark red blood are treated the same way in the field.

1. Direct Pressure (gloved hand)
2. Tourniquet (if applicable)
3. Pressure Bandage

Then more direct pressure!

Airway

It is not uncommon for a wounded patient to pass out due to blood loss, which lowers their blood pressure. When they pass out, they can block their own airway and thus we need to maintain it by placing a nasopharyngeal airway in their nose (that's where the Surgilube® comes into play.) You won't get this training in the Red Cross class but you will get it in the Dark Angel class. This tube allows air to get into the lungs upon a respiration when the mouth is closed or affected by trauma. If you don't have a trauma kit handy, then handle it by turning their head to the uninjured side and taking your first two fingers and scooping out any debris that they might have obstructing good airflow.

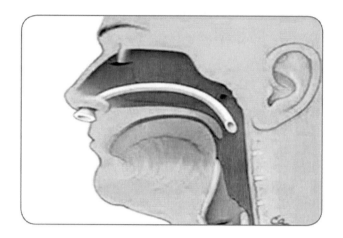

Tension Pneumothorax

A gunshot wound to the chest is a penetrating wound. There is a danger of air leaving the lung upon respiration and entering the pleural space (essentially the sack containing the lungs). When this happens, the lungs cannot expand upon inhalation and thus the victim suffocates.

We can relieve this by using a 14ga 3.25" needle and sticking it into the patient's chest, providing an escape for the trapped air. Yes, this is pretty high speed and may make you queasy, but it's a hell of a lot better than the feeling you'll get standing beside a casket! Again, you won't get this training at the Red Cross class, but you will get it in some advanced training classes.

While this is a brief explanation on the required training, kit, and treatment, it should bring to light an area where we all can expand our knowledge. I want you to be prepared for whatever this world throws at you. Handling bleeding and breathing is another skillset you need to have. If you carry a gun then you are carrying a trauma kit—inducing trauma, that is. Ensure that you can be within reach of your other trauma kit—the trauma reducing kit! I recommend that you make several trauma-reducing kits or purchase prepackaged kits from a reputable source.

A Note from EJ...

Buy or put together a trauma kit. Get certified in CPR and First Aid for adults and children. Take additional training classes that focus on bleeding and breathing. Become confident that you can save a life. You might have to save your own some day!

The fight is won or lost far away from witnesses behind the lines, in the gym, and out there on the road, long before I dance under those lights.

—Muhammad Ali

11

Training

Anyone who thinks that in a real gunfight that you are going to handle your firearm as you do when you train on a static range is sadly, even badly, mistaken. Training for a gunfight means building the emotional, mental, and physical skills you need to survive if you are ever in an armed confrontation. Unlike the couple of hours in a concealed carry permit class, successful gunfighting skills require hours of proper training. Once trained, maintenance of those skills requires repetition under realistic and dynamic conditions to induce a reasonable amount of stress to keep those skills sharp and your technique strong.

Movement, Repetition, Speed, Consistently in Technique, and Stress are requirements for training for a gunfight.

Carry

Obviously, if you live in a state that requires a permit to carry a firearm out in public then do what it takes to get that.

In many states it is a requirement to take a state-certified class on firearms as part of the qualification to carry process. These classes, generally speaking, cover the safety rules, basic handling procedures, state laws, and qualifying on a basic course of fire. It is imperative to learn about the laws and the civil liabilities involved in shooting another person to defend yourself and these courses can give you a basic understanding. States all have different requirements, as well as differing regulations on where you can and cannot carry. So learning and living by those are of utmost importance.

Gunfighting Rule 1
Bring a Gun!

Training to Fight

If you are new to the shooting community, then first start with a good fundamentals of shooting class from a reputable instructor. Depending on your ability and time constraints, you may need to take several of these courses and work offline in order to build good technique and instill proper gun handling skills. Once you have the fundamentals down, then you are ready to start learning basic and advanced shooting techniques and weapon manipulations that could give you opportunities in a gunfight for survival. There are many good shooting schools across the nation so look for one in your area. Also, several instructors/schools travel, so don't forget to look for a class that might be hosted near you.

Safety First

You have to commit to memory the following safety rules and incorporate them into your everyday life. Teach them to your children, your wife or husband, your friends, significant other, anyone who will listen!

4 Firearm Safety Rules:

1. Treat every gun as if it is loaded.
2. Keep your finger off the trigger until your sights are properly aligned and you are ready to shoot.
3. Never let your muzzle cross anything you are not willing to destroy.
4. Be sure of your target and what's in front and behind it.

Master the Basics

You will need a good foundation of basic marksmanship skills. Advanced shooting skills involve solid applications, and in some cases, modifications, of the basic skills and in order to do that you must start with mastering the basics.

You need good instinctive shooting (also referred to as "point shooting" by some instructors). Armed confrontations and gunfights typically happen in seconds. You need to be able to draw (most likely from concealment) and shoot multiple targets accurately. Then, you need to be able to do this as fast as possible.

Gunfighting Training Rule 1
Accuracy first, then speed!

You need good shooting from retention skills. Most gunfights happen at close distances and you will more than likely be fighting one or more assailants coming toward you. You will need to hold onto your gun tightly while firing multiple accurate shots.

You have to move! You're going to move. One way or another, you are going to move! Hopefully, you are moving offline of the attack and not down to the ground because you took a heat round. You need to incorporate movement into your training! A person who stays still is an easy target, and in fact, may end up lying still in a box. Conversely, the person who moves rapidly is more likely to survive the fight.

Gunfighting Training Rule 2
Move while practicing because that is most likely what you will do in a real gunfight!

Instructors

Seek out instructors from both the competition world and those who have been involved in real world action. My mother has a saying that has stuck with me all my life— "Take the good and leave the bad." With all the classes that you are sure to take, there will undoubtedly be tactics and skill-based techniques that just don't work for you. That's okay! Take what does work for you and leave the other in your toolbox for later consideration or as a conversation piece on poker night. Select tactics, techniques, and equipment that work for you, but pay special attention to the proven combat techniques from both the military and tactical law enforcement applications. Remember, it doesn't have to be sexy...it just has to work.

Physical Fitness

Beyond shooting, physical fitness is also critical to survival. The better shape you are in, the faster you can move and the less likely you are to get hurt. I watch too many individuals today rely on their weapon and ancillary "Gucci Gear" to solve all the problems. The issue with this is that you have to move that weapon into a solid shooting position not once, but multiple times during an engagement. This requires strength, stamina, and endurance. Many folks do not have the physical conditioning to get to or stay in the fight. That next area of cover may seem like ten miles away if you are out of shape. Also, think on this…your physical fitness level may be the determining factor as to whether you can keep your loved ones safe when the lead starts flying.

Realistic Training

I hammer home the use of cover to all my students. Brick walls and dirt stop bullets better than your house walls and car, believe it or not. Many of the competitions that I have watched or participated in have the shooter exposed to multiple targets during the course of fire. This is okay for the game, but if you overexpose yourself to multiple opponents, they can all shoot at you.

If they are shooting at you then you will probably be seeking cover rather than shooting back. Learn to engage and expose yourself to one threat at a time. Make the bad guy give you a full body shot to engage while you only give him your shooting eye and weapon. Don't get caught flatfooted in the open. In short, make yourself a hard target.

Gunfighting Training Rule 3
Maximize the use of cover; minimize your exposure.

Realistic tactical training may not feel rewarding at first. There are no prizes, certificates, or trophies to be had. The reward is being able to solve a deadly problem quickly and efficiently in your immediate space. The other reward is being able to go home at the end of the day and give the spouse a kiss and put the kids to bed.

Shooting or a Gunfight

Shooting is a one-way event. You do all the shooting! A gunfight is a two-way (or more) event. You do some of the shooting while someone shoots too. The difference between a gunfight and a competition is that the other shooter is shooting you—not at a paper target or a can on a fence.

Gunfights may lead to you getting shot and that is going to hurt! A lot! How do you make a "gunfight" into a "shooting"? Simple! See the threat faster, anticipate the next moves in the fight, and react more quickly than the other shooter.

Realistic training will put you in more "probable" scenarios to help you think faster and more tactically sound, should you actually be in a real gunfight. Your survival begins by setting yourself up in a tactically superior position before the fight happens. Control your opponent's OODA Loop and dominate the fight. Additionally, equipment, physical fitness, and overall mindset play critical roles in your success.

Up Close Targets

As for shooting and closing on a target, it only makes the bad guys' accuracy better. Walking into a muzzle may help you to test your newly found Superman powers sooner than you wished. Angled movement works, but again if you have to slow down too much, you are an easy target, and are generally in the open. Speed can act as your security in this case to get you to a point of cover.

Long Range Targets

Shooting at longer ranges helps establish proper sight alignment and trigger control. You have to take your time to line the shot up in order to hit the target. Once you can hit long range targets (twenty-five yards or more), you will see the front sight and the target area at closer ranges much clearer and your accuracy will improve.

All too often, I see instructors relying on some FBI statistic saying that the majority of gunfights take place at closer distances, therefore, they only train at closer distances. I would ask you to think about an active shooter situation where some scumbag has started shooting up a mall and he is across the food court from you. Can you hit him from where you are? Probably not! You have to train for it.

Shooting on the Move

Shooting on the move is a skill that all shooters aspire to learn and spend a great deal of time and effort trying to master. When moving at a careful hurry, you will find yourself stopping to plant your feet in order to make the shots.

When the bullets are flying, sprinting from cover to cover is moving too fast to shoot. There is no in between. If you slow down enough to make a solid hit when under fire, you are an easy target. So you have to make your decisions wisely. This is where Hollywood misleads you. They show slow-motion scenes of our hero advancing under a hail of bullets all the while making accurate shots and not getting hit. That's crap! You have to move quickly under fire, period! Get to cover then select your targets carefully and make accurate hits. Also, let me remind you that you do not have "unlimited" ammo like in Call of Duty. You will eventually run out so make your shots count.

A Note from EJ…

All of your training should be helping you to prepare mentally for sudden attacks and shooting under pressure. If you are not failing in your training drills then you are not pushing yourself hard enough. Amateurs practice till they get it right; professionals practice till they get it wrong. Master the basics and then work your way through the advanced skills keeping in mind—accuracy first and then speed.

Excellence is an art won by training and habitation. We do not act rightly because we have virtue or excellence, but we rather have those because we have acted rightly. We are what we repeatedly do. Excellence, then, is not an act but a habit.

—Aristotle

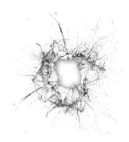

12

Preparing to Attend a Shooting Class

A ll too often, shooting classes are held up because that "someone" just isn't ready yet. That "someone" is still loading magazines (mags), still unboxing ammo, or because they just can find something. I have seen it all and I want to help you not be that "someone"! Here are the things you need to do during your preparation time, prior to attending a shooting class, so that you're keeping with the pace of the class and maximizing your learning potential. You paid good money to be there so let's keep you on the shooting line.

What You Need

Everyday Carry Pistol

First things first. You should train with the gun you are going to carry! All too often I see people using a Glock 17 (full size 9 mm) for the class only to put it away at the end of the training day and strap on a Glock 26 (subcompact 9mm). This is not doing you any good. If it is not what you are going to carry on an everyday basis, then don't train with it. Now, let me qualify this. If you are proficient on your everyday carry gun and are attending a course to become proficient on another gun, then it is fine to train on something besides your everyday carry.

Be absolutely sure you are good to go with your everyday carry first! If you carry a backup gun as part of your everyday carry, then wear and train with it too. What a great time to run that gun! Just let your instructor know before class starts that you want to use it and make sure they are okay with it. This won't be a problem with most instructors.

Spare Gun

I recommend you bring a spare gun to train with should your everyday carry gun go down hard. I have seen it happen several times. Luckily, the instructor let the person use his personal weapon or the range had rentals to use. Nothing can hurt your experience more than your smoke wagon taking a crap on you in the middle of Day 1.

Food for thought! You should also bring spare parts for your gun. If you don't have the knowledge or skill to replace it, don't worry. There are always people there that can help you, or your instructor should be able to get one of his guys to fix it for you while you use your spare. Again, this helps with your experience by keeping you on the shooting line.

Rifle

When you attend a rifle course, you should bring the rifle you are most likely to use in a personal defense situation. Your rifle should be zeroed prior to attending and that means the iron sights and cowitnessing the optic. Also, your pistol and rifle should be clean and well lubricated. All screws should have a drop of medium-grade Loctite® on them. Remember, you are going to run these guns hard and the vibration from the recoil will eventually loosen the screws. Then high-dollar items tend to give way to Earth's gravitational pull.

Magazines

The more magazines (mags) you bring, the longer you stay on the line. Don't just bring the two or three mags the gun came with. Most stoppages occur from bad mags. I recommend you bring at least six pistol and ten rifle mags, depending on the course you are attending. This goes for your backup and spare as well if they take different ones than your primary. Prior to class all of your mags should be loaded.

I have never seen an instructor get upset because one of his students had to unload. If, however, you show up without having mags already loaded, you have set yourself apart as that "someone" without ever stepping up on the shooting line.

Ammo

When attending a shooting class, bring good-quality ammo. Wolf Ammo for AK types and PMC or Federal bulk for ARs are always good choices. With pistol ammo, you have a lot of choices but if you are running a 1911 then use the ammo that *you* know will run without problems. Take all the ammo out of its packaging and dump them into an ammo can or box. Nothing irritates an instructor more, outside of a safety violation, than watching that "someone" open boxes of ammo and load mags.

So do everyone at the class and yourself a favor and just bring an ammo can full of loose ammo. If your buddies want to grab one of your mags and help you load then they just reach in your ammo can and grab a handful of ammo. This really speeds up the process of getting back up on the shooting line. If you need a little extra help in loading or you just want to save your fingers, then purchase and bring with you a Tula loader (you can thank me later!).

Cleaning Kit

Bring a well-stocked cleaning kit and extra lubrication and grease. The cleaning kit you might not need to use but if you don't bring it you *will* need it. The lubricant should be easy to apply and readily available. Also, just as important, bring a multitool or a tool kit with Allen wrenches. Things come loose and you will need tools to tighten them back up. If you are using an optic that requires a special tool (i.e., Aimpoint Micro), make sure that it travels with you to the range everyday of class. Bring extra batteries for your optic too! Murphy is hitching a ride with you to class and he decides when he wants to play, so be prepared.

Eye and Ear Protection

Eye and ear protection are a must. If you are using eye pro that has tinted lens then bring the clear ones too. A small cleaning rag is a good idea because they are going to get dirty from sweat and dust. I highly recommend electronic hearing protection, like Comp-Tacs®, because you are going to find it hard to hear if you are down on the end of the shooting line. Instructors tend to hang out near the middle of the line and you will struggle to hear if you bring the ear muffs your dad gave you to cut the lawn with. When you bring electronic hearing protection, bring extra batteries for them too! Remember, Murphy hitched a ride with you!

Medical

As with every trip to the range, you should bring a first aid kit (Band-Aids®, ointment, etc.) and a trauma kit (gunshot blowout kit). The trauma kit should have at least a pressure bandage and tourniquet in it. This way, if you get shot or shoot yourself, there is something to treat you with until the ambulance arrives. I pray that never happens to you but...

Extras

Your holster, belt, and extra mag carrier should be the same one you are using in your everyday carry. Showing up in the latest Call of Duty gear has no practical purpose if that is not your duty gear, yet there will be several that show up looking like they are CoD Prestige Level 4. I've seen it time and time again. You will see a desk jockey by day and a DeltaSEALRanger Command Private Major in class. I just chuckle to myself! Regardless of what you bring, make sure to test fit it all and simulate the movement you will perform in class. Make any necessary adjustments before you leave home.

Go ahead and pack everything the packing list says to bring because the instructor has a good reason why it's on there, so don't question it. The weather has a way of changing when you are stepping onto the shooting line and it pays to be prepared. If the packing list doesn't say to bring sunscreen and bug spray, bring it anyway. Mother nature is queen and you could become her court jester if you don't. Dehydration and fatigue are ever present. Bring a cooler full of ice and bottled water. Bring snack foods. Power bars, granola, and some candy for sugar are good choices. Go ahead and purchase a case of bottled water. Throw it in your vehicle to resupply your cooler throughout the course.

Prepare yourself for the class. Get in the best possible shape you can in the time you have before the class starts. You want to be able to complete all the drills without hurting yourself. Also, bring knee pads and elbow pads. You may not need them, but then again, you might just save those $200 Kryptek® pants you bought.

As with every gun owner I meet, I always recommend reading Colonel Jeff Cooper's book *Principles of Personal Defense*. It is the ultimate authority on the defensive mindset. You can read it in about an hour or less. It is life changing!

Now get out there and go train!

Few men are born brave. Many become so
through training and force of discipline.

—Publius Flavius Vegetius Renatus

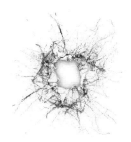

Closing

Starting in Genesis when Cain killed Able, violence has been a part of our lives. It haunts millions of families that have lost loved ones due to it. We can't escape our very nature. We can, however, defend ourselves from such violence by harnessing the intelligent animalistic nature that lies inside each and every one of us. We are capable of counterviolence if the will is there. Violent attackers believe you won't fight back, that you will lie down and beg for your life as they ruthlessly take it away from you. You have people who depend on you, that need you, so you have to live. Your kids need their father and mother, your spouse needs you to care and comfort them. To let this animal take your life before your walk on this planet is over is senseless.

Fight! Fight for your sake. Fight for their sakes. FIGHT, FIGHT, FIGHT, and LIVE!

These animals that would do this to you care nothing of your family's needs for you. They want what they want and don't care how they get it. If you have the mindset, skill, and tactics, you have a fighting chance at surviving a deadly encounter and with proper training you can obtain it. It is imperative that you meet violence with counterviolence, and that you do it!

Frederick the Great had a saying that General Patton loved to repeat to his troops: "Audacity, audacity, always audacity!" You have to be audacious and aggressive toward the criminal. Some may say that audacious and aggressive are not in their character, but without them, these people (now victims) will likely be dead. You...well, you will live... live to see your daughter or son celebrate another birthday or perhaps walk down the aisle at their wedding. Please take to heart the subjects discussed in this book, as they are what I believe are needed to survive.

May God bless and protect you!

—EJ Owens

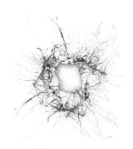

Appendix A

States with Castle Doctrine

Legislation Enacted in 2012

Alaska	Tennessee
Arizona	Mississippi
Idaho	Alabama
Montana	Georgia
Wyoming	Florida
North Dakota	South Carolina
South Dakota	Kentucky
Nebraska	Indiana
Oklahoma	Ohio
Texas	West Virginia
Missouri	Michigan
Louisiana	Maine

Reference:

http://www.concealandcarryhq.com/

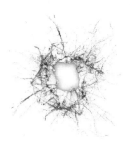

About the Author

E J Owens is professional firearms trainer, author, and consultant. His company Legally Concealed provides training to those responsible citizens who are legally allowed to use firearms for personal protection. EJ has served fourteen years in the army and Army National Guard and was an enlisted medic and finished his career as a commissioned infantry officer. He is a hand-to-hand combat instructor and a close quarters battle (CQB) instructor.

He has also served as a firefighter/paramedic for a major metropolitan fire department and was a Nationally Registered Emergency Medical Technician Paramedic (NREMT-P). He also served on the metropolitan medical strike team where he was trained in medical responses for nuclear, biological, and chemical incidents. He is also a certified rope repel master.

He is the 2009 Mississippi State IDPA champion/CDP.

He is a certified Glock armorer.

He has received multiple firearm instructor certifications to include the NRA and from legendary firearms instructor John Farnam.

He has an MBA and is the president of Legally Concealed. EJ currently lives in Memphis, Tennessee, with his wife, Jennifer, and his three children, Kaleb, Olivia, and Ethan.

Please check out EJ's other projects:

Videos:
Tactical Home Defense
Everyday Carry
Essentials of Gunfighting
AR-15 Crash Course

Books:
CounterViolence
A Life Worth Defending

Live Training:
Modern Warrior

Membership:
Sheepdog Society

These and other products can be purchased
at www.legallyconcealed.org.
Stay Alert and Practice Often! ™